Mrs D is Going Without

I used to be a boozy housewife.
Now I'm not. This is my book.

LOTTA DANN

ALLEN&UNWIN
SYDNEY • MELBOURNE • AUCKLAND • LONDON

First published in 2014

Copyright © Lotta Dann 2014

Allen & Unwin
Level 3, 228 Queen Street
Auckland 1010, New Zealand
Phone: (64 9) 377 3800

83 Alexander Street
Crows Nest NSW 2065, Australia
Phone: (61 2) 8425 0100
Email: info@allenandunwin.com
Web: www.allenandunwin.com

A catalogue record for this book is available
from the National Library of New Zealand

ISBN 978 1 877505 39 3

Quotes from *Women and Alcohol in Aotearoa/New Zealand* [report] on pp. 9–11
Jenny Rankine et. al. 2013 ISBN 978 0 9941021 2 6
Reproduced with kind permission from Alcohol Healthwatch and Women's Health Action

Table from *Controlling Your Drinking* (2nd ed.) on pp. 33 and 38
© William R. Miller and Ricardo F. Muñoz 2013 ISBN 978 1 46250 759 7
By kind permission of Guildord Publications, Inc.

Excerpt from *From Chocolate to Morphine* on p. 171
Copyright © 1983, 1993 by Andrew Weil and Winifred Rosen
Reprinted by permission of Houghton Mifflin Harcourt Publishing Company. All rights reserved

Quotes from *Kick the Drink . . . Easily* by Jason Vale on pp. 178–9 and 180–1
© Jason Vale 2011 ISBN 978 1 84590 390 9
By kind permission of Crown House Publishing Limited

Set in 13/17 pt Granjon by Bookhouse, Sydney
Printed and bound in Australia by Griffin Press

10 9 8 7 6 5 4 3 2 1

For the gorgeous men in my life—
Corin, Axel, Kaspar & Jakob

And to everyone who participates in the online
sober community—this book is for all of us

Introduction

I've written this book to tell the story of how I transformed myself from a miserable, boozy housewife into a self-respecting sober lady. What I've done is lay out in minute detail what I went through in the months leading up to my big decision to quit booze, and what transpired in the months following. I've provided an intimate look at what was going on in my mind; exactly how twisted my thinking was, how trapped and desperate I felt, how low I sank, how I made the decision to quit and, most importantly, what happened from that moment on. The personal revelations, the online community, all of it was unexpected and utterly fascinating.

I was one of those heavy drinkers where from the outside I didn't appear to be suffering. There were no clichéd signs that my drinking was a problem. This story doesn't contain wild drunken exploits or shock-horror tales of crazy debauchery. The police don't feature at all, there's no falling over in public, no waking up in jail cells or hospital beds. There are no crashed cars, broken glass, blacking out, pants wetting, fist fighting or drunken sex. The most I offer in terms of outward drinking drama is a few instances of vomiting, some embarrassing slurring and a bit of inappropriate loudness. I think most of my friends and family would admit that the biggest drama they experienced from me was when I announced I had a drinking problem and was giving up. And even to this day I'm sure there are a few people around me who are a little bemused that I've stopped drinking.

I can't blame them for that. I was the classic high-functioning boozer. Outwardly running a successful life but in truth managing a very dysfunctional, heavy, steady wine-drinking habit. For all intents and purposes I was an ordinary, hardworking housewife and mother, yet I was completely addicted to wine and on most nights was habitually filling myself up with far too much of the stuff. But make no mistake: while things might not have appeared outrageous from the outside, on the inside it was drama central.

My story is one of inner turmoil, a sick, twisted obsession, lonely angst, utter powerlessness and guilt—terrible guilt that gripped me, tormented me, and ultimately saved me.

What I went through in the lead-up to September 6, 2011, and what has transpired since that day, from my perspective, has been about as monumentally, earth-shatteringly intense as you can get. Drinking wine steadily and heavily for most of my adult life had slowly stripped me of my self-respect and trapped me in a deep, desperate misery.

This is what my story is about—my inner shit-storm as I came to grips with an alcohol addiction and then worked to turn my life around.

I had no idea what I was about to put myself through when I decided to stop drinking. I know now from having read numerous other stories through the blogging world that what I've been through since getting sober is entirely typical, but I had no clue at the outset. Getting sober took me through an entirely unexpected sequence of events, endless astounding revelations, surprising feelings and fascinating insights. I won't gild the lily—at times, especially early on, it was bloody tricky and rough, but there have also been truly wonderful and amazing phases. And now from my solidly sober position I can see that, inch by inch, through grit and tears, as I learned to live without wine I was lifting myself up.

From where I sit now (and I can hardly believe I'm going to say this considering where I've come from) I can tell you it's not the end of the world to live alcohol-free. It's honestly not. I don't touch alcohol *ever* anymore and it's totally and utterly fine. That's the simple truth. Of course, why and how I stopped drinking is incredibly complex, as it is for all of us ex-boozers, and it's taken hard work for me to get to this point, but that simple truth is what I sit with today: I don't have any alcohol in my life and it's totally fine.

It's better than fine, actually, it's fantastic.

Since I took the alcohol away on the 6th of September 2011, slowly but surely every aspect of my life has gotten better. This really is super-cool, especially given that things didn't appear particularly bad from the outside when I was boozing. Only after I put down the wineglass did I start to realise what a big impact my habitual drinking was having on all corners of my life. What emerged for me after I got sober was totally unexpected.

It's a fact: taking alcohol away has improved me. Now, almost three years after my last drink, I'm aware of so many improvements to my life. I sleep better, I eat better, I look better, I perform daily tasks better, my personal relationships are deeper and more authentic, including (probably most importantly) my relationship with myself. I respect myself now and trust myself. I'm not saying everything in my life is perfect all the time; that would be stupid, and of course it's not. But the majority of the time I feel calm, comfortable and in control. This is in such marked contrast with the sloppy behaviour, inner turmoil and angst I used to live with when I was boozing, not to mention the guilt and regret. In many ways I have simplified my life immensely by deciding to live without alcohol and even though that decision has taken me on a crazy rollercoaster ride, it's been so worth it.

I'm not unique in experiencing this sober transformation. Again, through following numerous other sobriety stories through the blogging world, I can see that feeling much better about yourself after getting sober is typical. I regularly witness as others dig deep, remove alcohol, get sober and experience uplifting transformations. It's really fun to watch and cheer on from the sidelines. And it always happens: if we stick at it and don't touch alcohol, the positive transformation comes. It always does. It takes grit and determination but eventually we reach solid sober ground and, trust me, it's a mighty fine place to be.

I don't regret all the boozing, lushing-out and overindulging that I've done throughout the years. To sit and regret strikes me as a huge waste of time (and I've been fortunate that my drinking never led to devastating consequences). If I hadn't done all the boozing that I have, I wouldn't have been able to experience the amazing uplift that being sober has given me. In a twisted way, I'm thankful for the boozing because it has given me the rich gift of sobriety.

It's also led me to this place in my life where I get to write and communicate daily with a wonderful, wise community of like-minded people. This is such an unexpected joy in my life. I had no idea that starting a blog would lead me into a place of such warmth and support. As I spell out in this book, I thought when I decided to start blogging as a way to keep myself honest that I was writing a private diary that would be tucked away in a corner of the internet, never seen by anyone. That people started reading and responding to me was so cool! The connections made through comments or emails feel real and strong and true, because they are real and strong and true. They might be dotted around the world, tucked away behind their computers, but the people who participate in the online sober community are real people. And the ones I hear from are unfailingly lovely; never judgemental, always supportive, always kind. They are also brave, determined and honest. It is truly amazing what goes on in the sober blogosphere.

I think finding support with not-drinking through the internet is the newest, most modern form of recovery, and it's growing daily. New blogs and websites dedicated to sobriety are popping up every day. Internet recovery is all the rage, and what's not to love about it? It's safe, it's kind, it's wise, it's warm, it's real. From the safety of your own home, you can reach out and connect openly and honestly with others in a similar position—worrying about and facing up to alcohol problems. Anyone can join in. You can read other blogs and comment, you can start your own blog and share your journey, you can use your real name or a fake one, or you can just lurk (read privately and never comment). It doesn't matter how you choose to participate in online recovery, so long as you know you are welcome.

I set out to get sober alone, and perhaps that was foolish—I'll never know, because I didn't stay alone for long. Support came to me through my blog fairly early in the process. Boy, was that exciting! I grasped that support with both hands, lapped it up, and fed it back at every opportunity. I took and I gave. People propped me up, I propped other people up. It may be (mostly) faceless and virtual but it is real. It is tangible and real and powerful and good and it has got me to this place of solid sobriety.

That's where I am now, firmly grounded in my new sober lifestyle. I don't live in fear and misery. I don't walk around worrying that in a weak moment I might decide to have 'just one' and suddenly find myself falling back down into a boozy hell-hole. I know I can never have 'just one' and, frankly, I don't want 'just one' anyway. Even if I were told today that I could suddenly, magically, be a moderate drinker again, I wouldn't pick up alcohol. If I were told today I have an incurable illness and only six months to live, I wouldn't pick up alcohol. Why would I bother bringing alcohol into the picture again after having done all this hard work in order to experience complete freedom from it? I don't want alcohol in my life; don't want it, don't need it, don't miss it. I don't think it has anything to offer me that I don't already have. I have fun, I have laughter, I have sadness, I have joy. I have real, authentic actions and reactions and that . . . that is bloody awesome. I am truly free from my alcohol addiction.

One of the best things for me in getting sober has been realising I can hold on to the parts of my personality I thought drinking was vital for—my sociability and my desire to be upbeat and have fun. Not drinking alcohol doesn't make me a geek. It doesn't make me boring. It doesn't mean I'm a loser. Not drinking alcohol doesn't mean I can't go to parties and dance all night or partake of long, lush lunches. It doesn't mean I can't talk crap with friends into the wee small hours or dance around my kitchen to cheesy pop tunes. It doesn't mean anything other than I don't drink alcohol.

I choose to not let the fact that I don't drink alcohol change the way I move and interact in the world. By and large I do everything the same as I did before, except I do it without drinking a brain-bending liquid. Okay—sometimes I might leave a party earlier than I would have before, or not go at all if it's an event I'm not particularly attached to. But for the most part I move and interact in the world much the same as I did before September 6th, 2011, except for the glorious little secret I have tucked away of how fundamentally improved I feel. It really is a big turnaround for me to be at this place after having been tightly locked in a habitual drinking habit.

I don't think my high-functioning boozing story is uncommon. I believe there are many thousands of people like me who are doing well in their outward life but in truth are regularly sinking far too much piss and always feeling guilty about it. Constantly through my online interactions and in my own circle of life, I hear from people who secretly worry about their own drinking. No doubt I'm hearing this because I'm openly sober and honest about why ('I don't drink because I can't control it' is my oft-repeated line), but my anecdotal evidence is matching up with the official line being touted. A new report called *Women and Alcohol in Aotearoa/New Zealand* confirms we're experiencing a significant shift towards heavier alcohol use among women and a rise in alcohol's harmful effects. The list of harmful effects isn't pretty: 'Alcohol-related harms for women include financial vulnerability, diminished physical and mental health, an increase in the severity and prevalence of violence directed at them, unplanned pregnancies and compromised parenting, family breakdown and erosion of cultural values and wellbeing.'

That's a short list but, holy shitballs, look at it again and read it slowly. It's actually a ginormous fireball of harmful effects. And so much of it I can relate to. Financial vulnerability? Can't believe what I used to spend on wine each week. Diminished physical health? Yep, and it only would have gotten worse if I'd kept guzzling. Compromised parenting? I'm sure there must have been a lot of that—hard to give your best at 7 p.m. when you're blurry with wine, or at 7 a.m. when your head is throbbing. Erosion of wellbeing? Oh yeah, I had that in spades. That term actually makes me feel like crying. That's the clincher right there. Towards the end of my boozing, when I was at my lowest ebb, my state of mind was shit. My wellbeing was well and truly eroded. That's what was killing me.

My steady, heavy boozing over years and years had slowly chipped away at my sense of wellbeing. One drink at a time I was shafting myself. I had no idea that's what I was doing. I thought drinking was cool and fun! I couldn't see what a negative impact it was having on me. It happened so gradually it was impossible to step back from the situation and see it for what it was. Only now that I've taken the alcohol away and experienced the incredible improvement to my life can I clearly see.

Today my sense of wellbeing is sky high. It's like the little fire inside me that I've been dulling for years with wine is finally being allowed to burn bright.

So why are we boozing so crazily? Why do so many of us rely on 'mum's juice' to get us through the days, itching for 'wine o'clock' to roll around so we can reach for our beloved liquid cope-all? The *Women and Alcohol* report offers a possible explanation: 'Women today balance the stresses of multiple roles, including family and childcare responsibilities, paid employment, and community and voluntary activities.' The pressures on men are just as great. But is this why I drank? Was I the classic example of the stressed-out, multitasking, high-achieving woman running herself ragged to try and do it all?

Here's another possible explanation for me from the report: 'Some young women perceive drinking as a sign and result of gender equality, as well as a way of restricting traditional constructions of femininity.' Was this part of the motivation for me when I started drinking at fifteen? Did I want to feel strong and equal? I always did like to prove my independence. Was drinking a way for me to feel powerful? If so, then how deluded I was.

Alcohol doesn't make you powerful. It diminishes your power. Particularly in situations where every inch of power a woman has, she needs. Consider these devastating lines from the report: 'Women who are sexually assaulted while affected by alcohol tend to blame themselves more, drink more and have more alcohol-related problems after the assault' and 'If the woman was drinking at the time of the assault, it can lead to guilt or self-blame, inhibit access to justice and increase her potential for alcohol abuse.' Diminished power indeed.

I doubt I'll ever know exactly why I became a hopeless boozer. There were so many contributing factors: my personality, my desire to keep things fun, wanting to appear 'cool' and strong, my dislike of negative emotions, my physical constitution, my fondness for inebriation, my inability to moderate, life events, environmental factors, this, that, the other. Whatever the reason (or reasons), it actually doesn't matter. The fact is, I am a hopeless boozer, and what matters is that I take full personal responsibility for that. It had to come from me.

If someone had tried to talk to me about my drinking being a problem before I'd owned up to it myself, I would have told them to go jump in the lake. No one could have forced me to stop; I had to dig deep and be brutally honest with myself in order to drive change.

I drove that change by taking 100 per cent personal responsibility for my drinking problem. I didn't look to blame anyone else, I didn't look to change anyone else. It was all about me. And because I took full responsibility and *owned my truth*, I was able to own the decision to remove alcohol from my life. *Just as I take 100 per cent responsibility for my drinking problem, I take 100 per cent responsibility for my sobriety.*

Here's the brutal truth: I am an alcoholic. I'm one of the many millions of people around the world who cannot control the drug of alcohol. It's a bit of an unfair fact about life but there you have it, some people can control alcohol and some people can't. I can't, and so I don't touch it. That's just the way it is. For those of us who cannot control it, there is no option but to just take it away. Just stop drinking alcohol and accept that you can never drink it again.

Well . . . I suppose there are other options. Us hopeless boozers could keep the alcohol in our lives and spend years angsting about why we can't drink normally, feeling guilty about hardly ever being able to rein ourselves in, trying a variety of techniques to control booze (limiting drinks per session, abstaining for periods, fixed days off, etc.), worrying, feeling like shit, not respecting ourselves and just thinking, thinking, thinking about alcohol all the time.

Or another option could be that we decide to just live as boozers and booze, booze, booze until the day we die. That choice is also available.

But for those of us who are sick of the boozing, and sick of the angsting and the guilt, we just have to be honest, take the drink away and learn to live without it. I did it, and thousands of others have, too.

I used to look at sober people and want to ask: 'What's it like? What's it like not drinking alcohol ever?' And now I can see how that is such a difficult question to answer. On the one hand, removing booze is monumental, a hugely life-changing, revelatory move to make. On the other hand it's just another decision made, change implemented, choice taken. I'm oversimplifying sobriety massively here but, at its most basic level, this is the truth.

I think if we make a decision to do something like remove alcohol from our lives, if we work really hard to follow through with that decision, gritting our teeth through the excruciating challenges, slogging away sluggishly through the lows, then adjusting and coping and managing to do it, over time we start to realise we have the power to direct our own lives (and that we've been lied to all these years and alcohol is not a necessary ingredient for a fun, full life).

And as long as we keep up with the not-drinking, slowly but surely we will experience an uplift. It is guaranteed.

Whatever your level of addiction, or the extent of your dependence, or your chosen path in attempting to live sober, know this—we can live without it. Regardless of what the liquor industry wants us to believe, we can live without alcohol—it is not a vital part of life, it is not the golden ticket to fun, it is not your friend. If you are sick of the boozing and sick of the guilt, know that it is entirely possible to take alcohol away and learn to live without it. If I can do it—me being completely convinced that booze was a necessary part of life—anyone can. Get whatever help you need. Find your community. Do whatever you need to do, but get rid of it. We can live without it.

I'm not ashamed of my drinking problem. Alcohol is addictive, everyone knows that. I'm not weak or a bad person because I got addicted to something that is addictive. I'm not going to hide my addiction and, more importantly, I'm not going to hide my recovery. If I can show what it was like for me learning how to live without alcohol, hopefully more people will see what the road is like: rocky at first, but beautifully smooth after a while. If one person stuck in a boozy nightmare instigates their own amazing transformation because of what I'm sharing, I'll be a very happy camper.

So here it is, here's my story. Here's what I went through as my drinking escalated to the point where I had to stop, and the amazing ride I've been on since that point of change. Step inside my mind, strap in and prepare for a bumpy ride, because it did get very bumpy . . .

1

December 2007

Holy shit, we're relocating! My husband Corin has landed a fabulous new job at TVNZ as the morning business presenter so we have to move to Auckland, where the studios are based. It's crazy busy and I'm flat-out organising everything. I've got lists for Africa. We've got a tight timeframe and Corin is already frequently flying up to Auckland to learn the ropes, so he's out of the picture. But that's okay—I'm an organisational whiz!

I'm wrapping up our lives in Wellington with ruthless efficiency. Doctor and dentist notes are being gathered. Belongings are being sorted and packed. Affairs are being ordered. Beloved caregivers are being bought gifts and showered with praise. Barbecues are being held to farewell friends and family. Tears are shed, but not mine—I'm too busy nailing it! Everyone is most impressed with how well I'm organising everything. But it's par for the course. I manage everything in my life extremely well. No one would expect anything less.

I'm drinking my way through the relocation, of course. Lots of red wine or chardonnay (anything but sauvignon)—a bottle a night, give or take. But hey, I never start before 5 p.m.(ish) and goodness knows I need it; I'm so busy and stressed. Anyway, it's normal, nightly drinking, and everyone does it, don't they? Five o'clock is wine o'clock, right? Okay, so I'm not sleeping a great deal, and kind of dealing with hangovers all the time, but so what? I'm a caring mother and a supportive wife, there's no problem here.

The hangovers aren't actually that bad, to be honest. At this stage in my life my body is a fine-tuned wine-processing machine. And so it should be by now, it's been used as such for the past twenty-odd years.

I first got drunk on Marque Vue aged fifteen, sitting on a beach in Banks Peninsula with a friend. We scoffed marshmallows while glugging the sweet bubbly wine. I later vomited up those marshmallows, whole, into an empty bath. It's one of the enduring memories of my youth—those undigested marshmallows, globs of pink and white spread across the bottom of the bath along with the rest of the contents of my stomach. Did that put me off booze? No way!

Nothing about the experience of that night, or any other days and nights that I drank through my teens, deterred me. Right from that first drunken night with the Marque Vue and the upchucked marshmallows, alcohol for me is like a fun challenge. It makes everything more interesting, more sparkly, more gnarly. Alcohol cranks up the dial, ups the ante, shifts the parameters of whatever is in front of me. I love it. I absolutely love it.

I love the fissure of excitement that passes around the room when alcohol is introduced. I love the anticipation of the fun and silliness to come. I love the dangerous taste of alcohol, the warmth of it as it slides down my throat, and the feeling as it spreads around my body; first in my belly, then snaking up my back and reaching into my head. I love the sensation of alcohol fizzing around my brain and sparking my nerve endings. I love how it loosens my thoughts, loosens my limbs and shifts my reality.

I've spent all of my years from the age of fifteen until now practising the fine art of getting pissed, navigating the boozed space in my mind, and having fun. I've drunk my way through journalism school and a career in TV news, travelling the world and lately settling down with Corin and having children. I've always managed to take a break from drinking for pregnancies and breastfeeding, but aside from those times drinking is an entrenched part of my lifestyle. It's what I do; I'm a drinker! Alcohol makes me feel comfortable and confident and naughty and (best of all) fun. Life is all about chasing the fun.

And luckily for me, even though I regularly drink, always steadily and sometimes heavily, rarely do I have black-outs and seldom do complete disasters occur. I manage to dance just inside the line of respectability, succeeding at jobs and managing relationships.

So now here I am in my mid-30s, married with two boisterous young sons aged just two and three years old, working part-time as a TV news producer, studying (a post-graduate diploma extramurally) and drinking my merry way through life. I'm a high-functioning, habitual boozer yet I consider myself a normal, ordinary gal with a normal, ordinary attitude to wine. Five o'clock is wine o'clock and, of course, five o'clock happens every day.

For boozy housewives like me 5 p.m. is a magical, mystical, crucial time of the day. It's the moment at which I open the bottle and escape the monotony. The kids' incessant demands become more bearable. I feel a little bit glamorous, a little bit naughty. I feel like I'm still part of the grown-up gang.

I never in a million years consider myself an alcoholic— god no! I'm not one of *those* people, those smelly derelicts lying in the gutter or scratching through rubbish bins. I'm a lovely, suburban, middle-class housewife, thank you very much! I don't hide vodka in a coffee mug in the morning; in fact, I rarely drink spirits at all. I don't stockpile booze

(I buy on the day what I will consume that night). I don't get the shakes and need a drink to make them stop. I don't black out and forget what happened. I don't wet my pants or sleep in my clothes. I'm well within the respectable line of drinking.

I think.

Lately, though, I've had this annoying, nagging realisation growing inside of me that my wine-drinking is getting kinda full-on. I'm sort of annoyingly aware that I'm always buying it, that I'm always drinking it. I'm annoyingly more aware that my hangovers are getting worse, and that *yet again* I feel sick in my guts from having had too much wine the night before.

This annoying awareness, this nagging knowledge, is forcing me to try and exert some control over my intake. Just lately I've been trying to limit the nights I drink, have regular dry-days or long periods where I abstain completely. I'm starting to have to put some effort into controlling my intake, and it's kind of annoying to note that it's bloody hard. I don't want to control my drinking. I love it! I love my nightly wines. I don't want to question my habit or dwell on the negatives; it's normal, I'm fun, I'm hardworking, I deserve it!

I try very hard not to dwell on the fact that I'm wobbly most nights. I try very hard not to dwell on the truth that my drinking habit is slowly but surely becoming quite serious. I try very hard not to admit the fact that I have a very determined, intense, obsessed and unhealthy dedication to wine . . . No, bugger that! No time for dwelling—onwards! I've got a relocation to organise. Corin's career is on the up. 'Get a bottle of red on the way home, would you, honey? Actually, make that two.' *Yee haa!*

I feel like this move to Auckland is a good thing for our family at this point in time. Our boys haven't started school yet and don't really care about much outside of their train set and toy cars, and of course that'll all move with us. Anyway, change is good. I embrace change. I'm easy-going, low-maintenance Lotta! Nothing really gets to me. I'm a cruiser, cruising my way to a new life in a new city. Let's go!

2

Three years later

Corin's been promoted! He's now one of the lead anchors on *Breakfast*. Every weekday he's out the door at 4.20 a.m. heading for the TVNZ studios to go live on-air for three hours. It's a very challenging and exhausting role but he loves it and we're all so proud. The boys and I are used to him not being around in the mornings and we're cool with that. I've got my routines down pat and everything runs smoothly. Of course it does. I manage everything extremely well, remember? Super-efficient, high-functioning me.

The mornings go like this: wake up, jug on, mug of instant coffee, painkillers, breakfast eaten, lunchboxes packed, kids dressed, me dressed, pack schoolbags, sunglasses on, out the door and into the day! I'm smiling and happy, even if my head aches. I breeze along. There's no problems here. I've made some fantastic new mummy friends in our community and our neighbours are all super-lovely. Life in Auckland is good.

We've produced another son since we've been here (three boys, can you imagine the noise levels in our house?!) and now he's one year old I'm back working as a TV news producer two evenings a week and have also recently enrolled to do a Master of Arts thesis part-time. Mostly, however, I think of myself as a housewife, and I love it! I care for the kids and Corin, I run the house, I manage the budget, I cook, I clean, I ferry everyone around. I even manage to exercise occasionally. And of course all of this crazy busy activity is accompanied by wine. I am busting my chops to be super-woman and do it all—be a wife, mother, worker, student, *and* a domestic goddess (ha ha)—all while maintaining a regular, steady wine-drinking habit. High-functioning to the max!

Every day at 5 o'clock the wine is opened. Like every other house in the country, right? We drink at least a bottle a night—to be fair, Corin usually only gets one or two small glasses but he doesn't seem to mind. By 8 p.m. the work is done, the kids are asleep and Corin's struggling to stay awake himself. The promise of a 3.45 a.m. alarm clock lures him toward bed and off he goes. Lucky me gets to sit up alone and indulge in as much reality TV as I like!

And more wine.

I'm vaguely aware that our new routine (with Corin now a shiftworker and usually heading to bed before me) is resulting in my wine habit becoming a little bit heavier. The wines I have while preparing dinner carry over into wine with the meal. The tidy-up-the-kitchen process that should really finish with my wineglass being put in the dishwasher doesn't. Instead I leave the glass on the bench and have another while bathing the boys and getting them into their PJs. Sometimes I carry my wineglass into the bedroom when I'm reading them a bedtime story. Often I'm filling up yet another glass when Corin is taking himself off to bed.

My part-time TV production work is carried out on Thursday and Friday, which is lucky for me because the 'Friday drinks' routine that was always around in my younger days is still in force and I get to load up for free in the office and kick-start my weekend. Bonus!

But as the months have passed in our new Auckland routine, I've been finding that one bottle of wine per day isn't ever quite enough. Lately I've been buying two a day on the murky pretence 'it'll last a while'. But it doesn't. Once I'm on the sofa in the evening in a quiet house with everyone else in bed, the TV on and a few vinos already in me, I find it very difficult not to keep heading to the kitchen for more. It calls to me—the wine—it calls my name; 'I'm over here, Lotta . . . there's a few more glasses left in me, Lotta . . . come and drink me, Lotta . . .' I find it very hard to say no.

So I pour just one more, just one more, just one more. My drinking habit is now a very quiet, private drinking habit. The blinds are down and no one can see me. I watch TV and make trips to the kitchen and the bathroom. Sometimes I make toast and eat four pieces at 10 p.m. like a freak. Eventually I slowly make my way to bed and crash out asleep. At this point, when I'm at my most sloshed, there's no one about. The family is all in a deep slumber. I don't need to form sentences. I don't even need to think very much. I'm not sure that I even realise how boozed I'm getting.

I keep painkillers in my bedside drawer and make sure I have a glass of water beside me so I can neck a couple as soon as I need to. I wake at 3 a.m. with my bladder full, my head pounding and guilt bouncing around my fizzy brain. Did I really need to have those last two glasses? Why didn't I stop earlier? Am I okay? Is this really still normal everyday drinking? Sometimes this fizzy 3 a.m. brain keeps me awake for a couple of hours. I don't want to, but I feel quietly miserable in those dark lonely hours.

For the most part all this drinking of mine is a solo pursuit, and as a result my growing concern is also mine alone. I try to talk to Corin about it but he doesn't seem to understand what I'm saying. He says things like, 'Yeah, I noticed you finished that second bottle after I'd gone to bed last night', and 'Just don't touch it during the week if you're that worried'. To be fair I'm a bit like Jekyll and Hyde when it comes to discussing my drinking. I can be completely open, vulnerable and honest about it one minute (usually in the morning when I'm hungover and feeling miserable) but if he tries to bring it up when I've got a glass in my hand I become very flippant, defensive and hostile to the whole discussion.

And, quite honestly, I really don't think he understands what it is I'm trying to tell him. He can listen to me, but he can't relate. He doesn't have the same twisted thinking that I do. His approach to alcohol seems fairly normal. Mine is not. I have a sick part of my brain that thinks about alcohol in a very obsessive and unhealthy way. I'm not what you could describe as 'breezy' about it. Mine isn't a 'take it or leave it' attitude by any stretch of the imagination.

I think about wine all the time. I'm concerned if there's not enough wine in the house for the evening. If we've got visitors I watch what other people are pouring and worry that there won't be enough left over for me. I tend to fill my glass to the top and slurp a bit down straightaway. I flip-flop constantly, feeling guilty one minute then planning to buy booze the next. I drink it in the evening with little regard for the fizzy 3 a.m. brain or hangover ahead.

My wine consumption is constant, but not always consistent—there are heavy phases and lighter phases. But the heavy phases, they're pretty bloody heavy and a lot goes down my throat. Here's what a typical heavy-drinking week would look like:

Sunday: Probably hungover from Saturday. Could possibly not drink at all. But perhaps get 1 bottle and have half of it. *Weekly total = ½ bottle.*

Monday: No hangover, so get 1 bottle and drink it. *Weekly total = 1½ bottles.*

Tuesday: Hungover. Get a bottle and drink half. *Weekly total = 2 bottles.*

Wednesday: Non-hangover day. Supermarket day. Buy 2 bottles, drink 1¼ bottles. *Weekly total = 3¼ bottles.*

Thursday: Very hungover. Get a bottle, perhaps have 2 glasses. *Weekly total = 4 bottles* (?? ish, it's getting hard to total).

Friday: It's Friday!!! Drink at least 1½ bottles of wine. *Weekly total = 5½ bottles.*

Saturday: Hungover. But who cares?! It's Saturday! Drink at least another 1½ bottles of wine. *Weekly total = 7 bottles.*

I seem unable to push aside my worry about my worsening drinking habit. There are two voices in my head. One is telling me boozing is fun and I deserve it and I'm totally fine. The other is telling me it's not fun, I don't deserve it and I'm not totally fine. I fluctuate from worrying for a week then not caring for a week. Worrying for a week then not caring for a week. Worrying, not caring. And all the while still drinking. It's madness! And no one knows about it, sees it or gets it, because from the outside I'm still a superwoman. High-achieving Lotta charging ahead with her life. I'm not having crazy drunken arguments with anyone. I'm not failing to achieve anything I need to achieve in my day-to-day life. Outwardly I'm fine. But I'm not fine. I'm drinking way too much.

My private, personal hell is at its blackest at 3 a.m. I come to consciousness in my bed, my brain is fizzy, my mouth is dry, my head is sore and my bladder is full. I walk miserably down the hall to the loo. I feel guilty. I regret. I just feel so unhappy.

I'm sure I don't seem as miserable to others as I sometimes feel. The misery comes and goes and it seems I can shove it to the side often enough to keep living normally and, most of the time, happily. Aside from my overly enthusiastic drinking habit, things are pretty good.

One long weekend we head to Napier to holiday with a bunch of Wellington friends that are driving up to meet us. We all book in to the Top 10 Holiday Park and spend three days drinking, eating, chatting, catching up, playing games with the kids, and just hanging out together.

It should be a fabulous fun weekend but it's not great for me. I have this insane notion that a holiday weekend like this has to involve a lot more drinking than normal. This is how I've approached holiday weekends all of my adult life, but now at nearly 40 I'm finding it hard to control the amount of wine I pour down my throat and keep it together.

The first night I try to create some kind of crazy, boozy, party buzz which really just means I get hammered and will the others to join in with my enthusiastic wine-drinking. There are a few others that hit it along with me but all in all the night is a gentle one and I feel a bit flat heading for bed that the night is over and was lacking in some way. Lacking? What the hell am I wanting? I have the people, the environment, the holiday, but I can't settle into that. I have to chase a boozy high. 'Must get drunk to have fun' methinks.

On the last night of the weekend I just go for it without caring that no one else is. Hell-for-leather drinking. I'm pestering others to get wine out of their units after ours has all gone. I'm talking total rubbish. I'm slurring. I'm noticeably trashed. I stumble into our unit at midnight completely and utterly written off. Crouch over the toilet vomiting, vomiting, vomiting. I lose a dearly beloved earring my sister gave me—is it down the toilet along with the contents of my stomach?

I wake up the next morning and put on a facade of being okay, all faux cheery and smiley as we pack up our unit and get the kids into the car. We wave goodbye to our lovely friends and drive for four hours home to Auckland.

It's an awful journey, I cry all the way. I feel unhealthy. I feel dysfunctional. I feel sad. I feel lost. And I have this nagging, gritty, burning feeling that things just aren't right here and something has to change.

3

Back home again I step up my efforts to try and control my intake. I get a book from the library called *Controlling Your Drinking* by William R. Miller PhD. It's full of questions for me to answer to help me figure out if I have a problem and frankly I feel good at being able to tick 'No' to so many of them: 'Do you ever drink before noon?', 'Have you gotten into fights when drinking?', 'Have you ever lost a job because of drinking?', 'Have you ever been in a hospital because of drinking?', 'Have you ever been told you have liver trouble?', 'Has your spouse (or other family member) ever gone to anyone for help about your drinking?' No, no, no . . . Phew. I feel reassured.

I decide anyway to try the author's moderation technique called 'Keeping Track'. For this I have to get a notebook and draw a table in it with intersecting horizontal and vertical lines. Across the top are the headings: Day, Time, Type of Drink, Amount, and Situation. Below there are numerous rows to fill in the details for each drink taken. I put my notebook in the bedroom drawer and on my first evening of 'Keeping Track' I run back and forth from the kitchen to the bedroom to fill it in.

There's a lot of running.

Day	Time	Type of Drink	Amount	Situation
Monday	4.57 p.m.	Red wine	1 glass	At home
Monday	5.17 p.m.	Red wine	1 glass	At home
"	5.52 p.m.	"	"	"
"	6.34 p.m.	"	"	"
"	7.14 p.m.	"	"	"

After the first couple of drinks I can't be bothered filling in most of the boxes and I abandon the whole thing after the first night. Too much bloody running back and forth to the bedroom! There's no big mystery to my drinking habit. I drink glasses of wine, at home, fast. I gulp. I devour. I practically inhale the sweet nectar.

I'm desperately clawing for the same feeling I had when I began drinking all those years ago. The same fissure of excitement when alcohol enters the picture, the same delight at the dangerously alluring taste. But slowly, deep down in the dark recesses of my brain, I'm realising that the fun in drinking is going for me. It's being replaced with a kind of focused determination. It's not uplifting anymore; in fact, it's kind of deadening. Heavier. Less fun. More miserable. And embarrassingly now, on the rare occasions that I'm drinking in front of others, I'm getting sloppier.

Corin and I go to a barbecue with his TVNZ colleagues. On arrival I cheerfully and gratefully accept a chardonnay from the hostess. 'That would be lovely, thanks!' As the barbecue progresses I continue to drink, perhaps just a tad too enthusiastically. I get a bit loud and opinionated. At one point in the evening I go to the bathroom and as I'm washing my hands I take a good long look at myself in the mirror and think, 'You are drinking too much, slow down.' I return to the dinner table and try to calm myself down, but en route home I feel uncomfortable about how I was acting. I know I was being overly chirpy and forced all night, not steady and calm. Not mature. Just boozy. Boozy me.

A few weeks later Corin and I have a rare child-free night out on the town. We start with a few drinks at home as we get ourselves ready and get the boys to bed. They're bouncing off the walls, excited knowing Mum and Dad are going out and a babysitter is looking after them. After a few extra bedtime stories (and wines) we finally manage to extract ourselves and head into town to a bar at the Sky Tower for cocktails and tapas. My brain tells me: 'Fun romantic evening! Must drink for the special occasion!' Drink I do. There are spirits involved. Bad mistake. Last stop of the night we head to a small underground bar where some DJ mates are spinning tunes. I'm quite drunk by this stage, and slurring. An old workmate comes over for a chat and I'm aware that I'm struggling to get my words out. It's excruciating, even I can see that from inside my drunk mind. After a short while he makes a bad excuse to get away from me, and I find myself sitting alone at the bar feeling drunk and embarrassed and strange and just wrong. This is all wrong. I find Corin and make him take me home 'right now, please'.

Fun romantic evening.

Then late one Friday at work my boss announces he's shouting dinner at the local bistro. We all have drinks in the office beforehand. Of course I manage at least three wines and drink them fast (I'm still locked in that mindset of free drinks in the office = must take advantage). We make our way to the restaurant, where I proceed to hit it even harder. Is everyone boozing away as merrily as I am? I have no idea. Possibly. I certainly am. Wine, wine, wine and more wine. By 10 p.m. I'm not really in control. I wobble to the toilet, spinning out. I must be pretty obviously drunk by now, but it's Friday night! Isn't everyone?! I make it into a taxi and concentrate very hard in the back seat all the way home. In my bent brain I realise I'm actually really fucking drunk. I manage to pay the driver and get inside, racing for the toilet. Now I'm puking in the loo. On my knees, in my work clothes, vomiting up my dinner. I'm nearly 40. I'm a happy, contented wife and mother. A working woman with it all going on. What am I doing here on the toilet floor, holding my hair back and vomiting up my steak au poivre? I think of Corin and our sons asleep down the hall and hope like hell they can't hear me. Hope they don't see me. This is not good. This is not normal, healthy drinking.

I beat myself up for the rest of the weekend (and my throat is sore from vomiting), but by Monday I've decided I'm going to drink again that night. The guilt gets pushed aside, and the more time that passes since the Friday night binge the more I see it as merely a rare blow-out and no big deal. Who doesn't have those? I convince myself it's normal for a middle-aged mother of three to end up on the toilet floor puking from too much wine, and I go on my merry way.

Of course, wine is still constantly on my mind. I start doing deals with myself: 'I won't drink much on Sunday night because I want to go to the gym on Monday morning. Then Monday night I can have a few because Tuesday isn't a gym day so it'll be okay to have a hangover. That hangover will stop me drinking too much on Tuesday night which is good because Wednesday morning I want to go back to the gym.' Sometimes the best-laid plans go awry and occasionally (or quite often) I find myself at the gym rolling my body over a swiss ball with my guts churning and my head throbbing.

I look at the ladies around me and wonder if anyone else is secretly hungover. I feel so miserable.

I'm conscious of every time I take a big gulp of wine at home. Standing at the kitchen bench. Sitting on the sofa. Over and over and over again I gulp wine. I seem unable to ignore what I'm doing. Can't anyone else see? I feel desperate and alone.

So I get really brave and phone the Alcohol Drug Helpline. I speak breezily and confidently to the woman at the other end of the phone line. 'I'm just wondering about what's normal?' I chirp. 'Is a bottle a night too much?' She's calm and gentle. I can tell she's letting me talk, letting me figure it out. 'I'm pretty sure I'm fine,' I chirp, 'but yes, you might as well send me some information.' I'm left feeling dissatisfied with the conversation. What did I hope to get out of it, I wonder. She wasn't very helpful, really, I conclude. But the truth lingers.

I called a helpline. I called an alcohol helpline.

The calm lady does as promised and some information arrives in the mail. Contained among the pages is another questionnaire designed to help me assess my drinking. It's far more pertinent than the questionnaire I did earlier, and as a result less reassuring.

Question 1: How often do you have a drink containing alcohol?

Answer: Four or more times a week (worst possible answer).

Question 2: How many standard drinks containing alcohol do you have on a typical day when you are drinking?

Answer: Hmmm. Well, this I'm not sure about, as I don't really know what constitutes a standard drink.

The helpline's information pack tells me. It says one standard drink of wine is 100 ml. I don't know exactly what that looks like, so I get my red plastic measuring cup from the kitchen drawer and fill it with water from the tap to 100 ml. Then I pour that into my wineglass. Holy shit! That's only around a third of what I normally pour! That means I'm having almost three standard drinks in just one of my glasses of wine.

I think back to my 'Keeping Track' table and how inaccurate my inputting was. It really should have looked like this:

Day	Time	Type of Drink	Amount	Situation
Monday	4.57 p.m.	Red wine	~~1 glass~~ 3 standard drinks	At home
Monday	5.17 p.m.	Red wine	~~1 glass~~ 3 standard drinks	At home
"	5.52 p.m.	"	"	"
"	6.34 p.m.	"	"	"
"	7.14 p.m.	"	"	"

Don't add that up, okay? Moving on . . .

Question 3: How often do you have six or more standard drinks on one occasion?

Answer: Daily or almost daily (worst possible answer).

Question 4: How often during the last year have you found that you were not able to stop drinking once you had started?

Answer: Daily or almost daily (worst possible answer).

Question 5: How often in the last year have you failed to do what was normally expected from you because of drinking?

Answer: Never. Well, phew! I get to click on the best possible answer here. I'm a high-functioning boozer, baby!

Question 6: How often in the last year have you needed a drink in the morning to get yourself going after a heavy drinking session?

Answer: Never, never, never! *Woohoo! I'm on a roll!* I'm starting to relax now; maybe I'm not that bad after all.

Question 7: How often in the last year have you had a feeling of guilt or remorse after drinking?

Answer: *Shitballs. I'm going to have to be honest here.* Daily or almost daily (worst possible answer). Damn that guilt.

Question 8: How often in the last year have you been unable to remember what happened the night before because you had been drinking?

Answer: Never. (Phew. No black-outs for me thankfully. Although sometimes I do find myself watching an entire episode of *Keeping Up with the Kardashians* without realising until near the end that I've seen the whole damn thing before.)

Question 9: Have you or someone else been injured as a result of your drinking?

Answer: No. (This is good.)

Question 10: Has a relative, friend or doctor, or other health worker been concerned about your drinking or suggested that you should cut down?

Answer: No! (Whoop!)

I finish the questionnaire feeling overall like I'm going to be okay. I tally up my score and it's 17 out of 40. Surely that's not too bad. But then comes the shock—the comment attached to my score reads: *Your drinking will cause you or may have already caused you problems.*

4

I shelve it. The information pack and questionnaire gets shoved in the hall cupboard and I decide to press on as normal. I mean, what exactly am I supposed to do with that knowledge anyway? *Will cause or may have already caused you problems* sounds way too severe, way too dramatic. I have no idea what to do with that so I shelve it and move on.

I do decide, however, to talk sternly to myself about my drinking and my need to moderate it, and so I write myself a note. Two notes actually, on two pages of a reporter's notebook. One I title 'Goodbye' and the other 'Hello'.

Goodbye

— *To the 'rebellious' Lotta*
— *To the Lotta who throws common sense out the window when it comes to drinking*

41

- *To the Lotta who ignores the inner voice that knows it is stupid*
- *To hangovers, headaches + sick guts*
- *To wasting time worrying and beating myself up about drinking*
- *Say goodbye to a need to GET HAMMERED every time I drink*
- *To telling myself 'stuff it, it's okay to pound it harder'*
- *Say goodbye to allowing the HUNGER for drink to dominate*
- *Say goodbye to thinking the only way to have a good time is by drinking LOTS FAST*
- *Say goodbye to the old Lotta*
- *Grow up, move on, embrace a different second half of your life.*

Hello

- *Say hello to the Lotta you want to be for the rest of your life*
- *Say hello to a Lotta who is grown up, reliable + sensible when it comes to drink*
- *Say hello to a Lotta who is happy to stop drinking when the feeling is enough (think about going to bed, sleeping + waking up in the morning)*

- *Think about that image of the person you want to be; who feels together, sorted*
- *Hello to a mother who is not going to cause her sons any worry or harm*
- *Drink slower. Enjoy it. Remember the effect is delayed*
- *STOP.*

I scribble the notes off quickly, rip the pages out, put them in my bedside drawer then dive back into my life.

And I try to moderate, I really do try. But you know, when that sweet nectar hits my throat and the tingles start around my body, when the warmth spreads from my backbone up to my brain, I'm lost. I'm a goner. I just love drinking wine. And so pretty soon I'm back into my same habits. My heavy-drinking Mondays, Wednesdays, Fridays and Saturdays, and my lighter drinking Sundays, Tuesdays and Thursdays. Pretty soon I'm looking for excuses to drink more (let's have a disco with the kids after school on Friday—I'll get the bubbles!) and am chatting to the man at the local bottle store about my studies. He knows about my life.

I love drinking, yet I hate it as well. I love it at 5 p.m. and fall more deeply in love with it as the evening progresses. I'm still loving it when I fall into bed around 10 or 11 p.m., but sometime in the wee small hours the love morphs into hatred and time and again I find myself awake at 3 a.m. burning with guilt and disgust. Come 7 a.m. and the guilt and hatred have turned into a deep misery. I put on a smile and get on with my day and by lunchtime the misery is lingering only slightly. Once the afternoon is underway the negative thoughts have all but disappeared and the longing and desire starts to grow again. And then it's 5 o'clock.

I'm locked in a ridiculous, vicious, nasty, insidious, twisted, sick, exhausting cycle of booze drinking. I am completely obsessed. I drink. I regret. I drink. I regret. I drink. I regret. I'm lost, drowning in a sea of vino and mixed emotions. And I'm lonely with it. It's a private miserable drinking hell and although I might try to draw Corin in, my split personality makes it incredibly hard for him to really help. The Jekyll in me—the worried person—cries and moans to him about my drinking, but the Hyde—the enthusiastic boozer—just wants to keep imbibing and shuts him out. I'm my own worst enemy and as a result my inner angst is largely mine alone.

Also, to be fair on Corin and the others around me, there's not a lot for them to point at. Outwardly my drinking, while clearly of the 'enthusiastic' variety, manages to dance just inside the line of social acceptability. Outwardly I'm still a busy, high-performing, high-functioning woman. I'm still running the household, mothering full-time, working on my thesis part-time, dragging my sorry ass to the gym a couple of times a week, maintaining friendships and a social family life. I'm sure if my friends and family were pushed they'd probably say, 'Yeah, Lotta likes her wines', but nothing more than that. I want our house to be known as a warm house—open and social and busy and fun. I love fun! And I love community. The more friends we have the better, I say, and what better way to entertain them than by popping a cork?

My brother-in-law comes to stay with us for a few weeks and after he returns home my sister tells me that he remarked, 'Every night's a party at their house.' I laugh the comment off and try not to admit that deep down it makes me feel uncomfortable.

A neighbourhood friend drives past our house on her way to school and on rubbish days often says to me, 'I see you guys had another good week!', in reference to our overflowing recycling bin. I laugh along with her and act like it's a badge of honour—*See how cool and fun we are!*—but secretly feel embarrassed that our huge pile of empties is so visible. I'm delighted when the city council changes the recycling bins to large wheelie ones with lids.

Inwardly and privately my drinking is anything but cool and fun. Somewhere in the past few years I've crossed over that blurry line between normal, healthy drinking into abnormal, dysfunctional drinking. No one else knows the full extent of my steady, heavy wine intake, nor can they hear the sick, obsessed voice in my head regarding the stuff. All of the patterns of behaviour and instances of regret are lining up only in my head. The chattering, mounting concern is only audible to me. It's my concern and mine alone, and even for me the concern comes and goes depending on what time of the day it is. I feel trapped and lonely inside my own sick, flip-flopping mind. How utterly fucked up this is.

Then one Friday evening we head up the road to visit some friends for an early meal with the kids. A small party of sorts for us hardworking parents. The adults all have a few drinkies while chatting and making pizzas and the kids have a disco dance with glow sticks then settle down to watch a DVD. It gets dark and the fireworks come out. We're all boozing. Is everyone boozing as fast as me? No idea. But I'm going for it. It's Friday night! I'm out! Wine! Wine! Wine!

I hit the vino so hard I can barely walk straight as we leave around 9.30 p.m. . . . It takes an immense amount of effort and focus to get the kids sorted with their shoes and coats. Corin carries our eldest on his back and I push the two little ones in the double buggy the two blocks home. I'm moving fast because I can feel my head spinning and my guts churning. I barely make it home before racing to the toilet to puke my guts out. Classy me once again on my knees heaving into the porcelain bowl. Inviting Ralph and Chuck to the party. Talking to the great white telephone. Whatever happened to saying goodbye to a need to *get hammered* every time I drink? What happened to saying goodbye to the rebellious me? What happened to saying goodbye to allowing the *hunger* for drink to dominate? What the fuck happened?

I decide a more drastic measure is required if I'm going to get on top of my boozing and so I resolve to completely stop drinking for a month. I've done this before after heavy-boozing periods and it always works to lower my tolerance and slow me down. A whole month off, I decide, will sort me out.

It's a tough month with me white-knuckling my way through. Some evenings at around 5 p.m. I'm so tense all I can do is sit on the sofa with a magazine and not talk to anyone. After two weeks I start fantasising about what I'm going to drink when I start up again. I make it to three-and-a-half weeks before I decide that's long enough and get back into it. It's Wednesday when I start drinking again and soon after I realise that this time my month off didn't have the desired effect. I'm already back to drinking at least a bottle a night. Friday I hit it hard. Saturday we have friends over to watch the rugby and I hit it hard again. I hit it so hard that before they even arrive at 7.30 p.m. I pause momentarily at the kitchen bench and think, 'I've got a whole bottle of wine inside me and I can hardly feel it.' It's a strange and uncomfortable thought but it doesn't worry me enough to stop me drinking.

I have no more wine in the house so I knock back a couple of Corin's beers then fidget and obsess internally until

I gain the courage to ask one of our guests if I can please have a glass from his bottle of red. I'm dimly aware of how unhealthy I am being, but there's no stopping this hunger I have to drink. I feel like I'm on a strange theme park ride that is hurtling me towards some unknown doom and I can't get off. Is it a rollercoaster where I'm simply strapped in the back and not in control? Or is it a racing car with me at the wheel and my own foot stuck on the gas? Whatever the case I'm speeding headlong deeper and deeper into a drinking madness. It's almost as if I'm willing myself there.

And so it is that I hurtle towards my last night ever of drinking.

5

It's Monday—just five days after my self-enforced break from the booze and already I have a heavy-drinking weekend under my belt. Yet again in the middle of the day I find myself wrestling internally over whether to buy wine or not. I'm trying to resist the urge and manage to do the school pick-up without going via the bottle store but by 4 p.m. I'm regretting not having any wine in the house. Finally I blurt out and ask Corin if he can go and buy some. He says, 'Nah, let's not bother, let's just have an alcohol-free day.' I murmur agreement but I just can't let it go. My brain is screaming 'wine, wine, wine, wine', so just after 5 p.m. when Corin leaves to take our two big boys to their Scouts meeting I pluck our youngest son off the floor where he's playing with his plastic animals and actually say aloud to him, 'Let's go prove how dysfunctional I really am,' and race to the car. I'm in such a crazy mindset that as I rush to back out of the carport I run over the new pram and smash up one of its front tyres. It's completely stuffed. And I haven't even had a drink yet. But still I go on. Once I'm at the bottle shop I grab two bottles instead of one: a white and a red.

Home I come and promptly scull most of the bottle of white while I bathe the Little Guy and tidy up the dinner mess. I even manage to run the vacuum over the living room floor, pausing often to slurp down another big gulp of wine. It's barely touching the sides. Heavy-boozing, high-functioning housewife me.

Just before Corin is due home, I panic. Shit! What's he going to think about me not sticking to an alcohol-free day? I feel embarrassed and frantic and in an instant I make a crazy snap decision—to hide the last skerricks of the bottle of white. I'm barely thinking straight, I'm a whirling dervish of boozy madness.

I grab the nearly empty bottle and crouch down on my hands and knees on the kitchen floor. I lean inside the pantry, right to the back of the bottom shelf, and tuck the bottle away behind the yoghurt maker and the spare boxes of tissues. Then I stand up, dust myself off, get out a new wineglass for Corin, open the bottle of red, pour each of us a glass and leave the bottle sitting plainly in sight on the kitchen bench.

I hid wine.

Corin arrives home and immediately spots the red wine on the bench and kind of laughs that I didn't manage to go without. 'Oh, you couldn't make it, eh?'

And I laugh too, 'Ha ha, yeah!', and make a song and dance about how I've not had much yet. 'I waited for you—see, the bottle is nearly full!'

I hid wine. I have never hidden wine before.

Over the next couple of hours Corin has maybe two small glasses of red and I polish off the rest. So most of a bottle of red wine goes down my throat to join the most of a bottle of white wine that I'd secretly drunk earlier. Another binge.

I hid wine. I got down on my hands and knees and hid a bottle to conceal how much I'd been drinking from Corin.

Eventually the evening ends and I fall into bed, drunk yet again. Where am I going with this behaviour? Where the fuck am I heading?

When Corin's alarm goes off at 3.45 a.m. I'm already in hell. He reaches out quickly to stop the noise and gets silently out of bed, propelled by the knowledge he needs to be in the studio and on TV in just over two hours and believing himself to be the only one who's awake at this ungodly hour. He pads quietly from the bedroom—his clothes already laid out on the dining room table as they always are so he doesn't have to wake me as he gets ready for work.

I hid wine.

I lie still in bed and don't say a word. My tongue is thick and my mouth is dry. My head is throbbing with an almighty headache and I'm being driven crazy by the voice inside my mind that won't shut up. My thoughts are spewing forth, a panicky jumble of frantic words.

Oh my god I can't believe you did that you are so dysfunctional you hid wine that is a step too far oh my god where are you heading I can't believe you lied to Corin what is wrong with you why did you have to drink so much wine last night there is a serious problem here you really are a loser you have a major problem you cannot continue down this path you can't control your drinking you can't control your drinking you can't control your drinking.

I lie there miserable, my thoughts taunting me, my bladder full, my guts churning and my head throbbing. After what seems like an eternity—but is only around twenty minutes—Corin has showered, had his tea and toast, and is sneaking out the back door to get in the car and drive to TVNZ to face the nation.

I hid wine.

Finally I get up to go to the toilet. This is absolute bloody bollocks, I think to myself as I sit on the toilet with my head in my hands. I am utterly and desperately unhappy and it is all of my own doing. It's me who is creating this misery. I'm the one who buys the bottles. I'm the one who twists the tops. I'm the one who pours the glasses. It's my elbow that I bend in lifting the glass time and again, and it's my throat that swallows the liquid. It's all me. As I sit in the dark I realise with absolute clarity that nobody else can help me. I create the pain, I'm the only one who can stop it. Not the woman at the end of the helpline, not Corin, not anyone else. Me. It's only me.

By the time the kids wake up I'm totally buggered. I've got an awful wide-eyed sleep-deprived feeling on top of an intensifying headache, churning sick guts and an overwhelming feeling of guilt and dysfunction.

As the kids bang and crash their way through their cereal (are they shouting on purpose?) and I bemoan the lack of painkillers in the house, the TV gets flicked on and up pops Corin on the screen. He's interviewing the prime minister. Corin looks great, all crisp and alert with his suit on and hair done, in his element talking about politics.

I stand at the kitchen bench watching my husband on the television at the other end of the living room. Honestly, it's like an out-of-body experience: I can see the scene as if through the lens of a movie camera. Me—the hungover dishevelled housewife, with bed hair, a dirty dressing gown, droopy eyes and miserable face. Corin—smiling, alert and focused on the television, asking pertinent questions. It's horrendous, my misery is deep and I feel very, very alone. I'm locked in my own private hell. My own private drinking hell. And I put myself here, I poured all the wine down my throat last night. I hid wine and lied about how much I'd had to drink.

I shudder, imagining what fans of *Breakfast* would think if they could see the truth of what Corin lives with at home. I think about how all the women's magazines have wanted to do feature articles on us since he became a TV presenter—the classic 'TV Star At Home With Lovely Wife and Cute Kids' story. We've always refused, not wanting to present an untrue fantasy version of ourselves to the nation, all styled and groomed and flawless. Well, if only they could see the truth, that Corin Dann's wife is actually a bloody loser lush who can't control her drinking.

I feel like crying. I'm fucking it all up. I'm an embarrassment to myself. Do I want to have this hidden problem, go on boozing and pretending that I have it all together, pretending that I'm superwoman, pretending that I'm not a problem drinker? Do I want to be this woman?

As the kids get dressed ('No, you can't wear your pyjamas to school!'), I crouch down on the kitchen floor and reach into the back of the pantry to retrieve the bottle I hid last night. I still feel like there is a camera on the ceiling watching my every move, so acute is my awareness of how utterly wrong this behaviour is. I pour what's left of the bottle down the sink (not much) and hurl the empty into the recycling bin. *I've had enough of this shit, goddamnit! I've had enough. This has got to stop. Now.* I grasp at the feeling that if I only have myself to blame then I only have myself to change and if it's only me changing myself then surely I can make that change.

I feel like I'm fighting desperately in the middle of a war and I'm losing. But it's a crazy kind of sick and twisted war because I'm on both sides of the battle. On one side is the me who knows my drinking is a problem and knows it's wrong and feels guilty and shitty and awful all the time. Then there's the me on the other side which is the me I turn into the minute I make the decision to drink and the alcohol enters my system. At that point I switch sides and start fighting back with myself, with a brain that is fuzzy and warm and under the influence. I'm at war with myself; it's me on me.

Yet there's this other enemy against me, another substance. Alcohol. Once I put alcohol in my body I jump immediately to the other side of the battle and start fighting back at myself. The problem isn't me, the problem is the substance. The problem is alcohol. Deep down I know that unless I remove the alcohol completely, I'm never going to win this war. I'm going to spend the rest of my days fighting a ridiculous, stupid, crazy, awful war. I have to be smart. I know that to win I must remove the alcohol. Remove the alcohol and the war is over.

But fucking fuck holy shit motherfucking fuck! This is alcohol, for fuck's sake! Who lives without alcohol? Alcohol is everywhere! It's an intrinsic element of our landscape; it's wedded into every aspect of our culture. It's part of life.

And not only is it everywhere but alcohol is a huge part of my own personal identity. It's been my constant companion since I was a teenager. I drink. I'm a drinker. I love to drink. I'm fun Lotta. I'm that naughty, up-for-it girl who everybody likes having fun with. It's who I am, for fuck's sake. Am I going to have to completely reinvent myself if I stop drinking? What if people don't like the new me?

What if I don't like the new me?

Glumly, I realise that I have no choice. Either I'm going to keep fighting this ridiculous war with myself, or I'm going to commit to being on one side of it forever by completely obliterating the other side, by removing alcohol and *never drinking again*. Alcohol is the enemy, not me. Alcohol is the problem, not me. Alcohol has got to go. Standing there in my dressing gown the thought comes to me: 'I could just do it and stop right now. I could just take that fucking leap and remove alcohol from my life.'

6

So that's it. I'm making the decision. Right here. Right now. In my dressing gown with my sore head. This is it. No more farting around trying to moderate and control. I've been doing that for a good number of months now—years even. And I've proved to myself time and time again that when it comes to alcohol I just cannot win. I've wrestled and fought and tried and tried and failed and failed to be a normal, moderate drinker and I just can't be her. So that's it. From this day forward I am never going to touch alcohol again.

Holy fucking shitballs. It actually feels like a giant anvil has just dropped from the sky and landed in my hungover lap. It feels monumental, mind-blowingly scary and completely unknown, but also entirely possible and somewhat exciting. Other people do this, why not me? Why not tragic, secretly boozy housewife me?

I manage to get my shit together enough to take the big boys to school (stay in car, sunglasses on, quick dash into the chemist on the way home for painkillers). Once home again I set up our youngest with some toys, take a piece of A4 paper out of the printer, find a pen and sit down to write another letter to myself. It's not yet 9 a.m. and *Breakfast* is still on air. Corin is interviewing a fashion expert about trends for summer. He's trying on hats. I can't even muster a giggle at knowing how uncomfortable he'll be feeling. I'm on a mission. I take the biro—it's red—and I write a letter to myself:

I am going to stop drinking forever.
I am not going to lose anything by removing alcohol from my life.
I am going to gain a lot!
I cannot control alcohol, it controls me.
I don't even have joyful + fun drinking anymore.
I cannot moderate.
Every time I drink alcohol I binge.
I suffer the next day and as a result the kids suffer.
Alcohol stops me being the best mother I can be.
Alcohol makes my life harder and increases negative thoughts.
I will be 40 soon and I need to stay in good health.
Today is September 6th 2011.
Today is Day One.
Go Lotta!
xxx

At 11 a.m. Corin arrives home from the TVNZ studios. I'm sitting at the dining room table, an exhausted, hungover, emotional wreck.

'Hey,' he says as he walks into the kitchen and drops his stuff on the bench.

'Hey,' I answer back glumly. There's a pause and then I start crying.

'What's wrong?' He looks concerned.

'I . . . (sniff sniff) . . . I have to stop drinking,' I say.

'Really?' he says. He looks a little taken aback but also not entirely surprised.

I blurt out the truth about last night. 'I lied to you,' I admit. 'I actually bought two bottles of wine and drank most of the first one before you got home. I hid it in the pantry.'

Corin looks at me for a while and then says quietly, 'You know, I kind of knew. You seemed quite full of wine when I got back.' Then he confesses: 'I actually had a sneaky look in the recycling bin to see if there was another empty bottle in there.'

Oh holy hell. What life of deception and secrets are we building for ourselves here? I have to stop this madness from going any further.

Something has changed in me, this time it's different. I can tell. My whole internal landscape has shifted. And so has my outlook. The world feels different. It feels monumental.

Corin and I talk for a bit and then he heads off for a nap. My brain is fizzing madly, thinking about what I'm intending to do and how exactly I'm going to do it. I head to the playground with our youngest (sunglasses still firmly fixed to face, pushing the swing in a lacklustre fashion) and on the way home, sitting at the traffic lights, I start thinking about the notes and letters I've been writing to myself recently. I decide it would be a good idea to keep going with that—to chart my thoughts and feelings, to help keep myself honest and on track. I still feel largely alone in my resolve. Corin is, as he always has been, unwavering in his love and support but, really, what can he do? Love and support is the best he can do and he does that wholeheartedly and unconditionally. The rest I need to do myself. I've always been alone in my concern about my drinking and now I'm alone in my newfound grit and determination. I need to constantly hear from myself as I head down this non-drinking road.

I ponder buying a notebook to keep beside my bed so I can jot down my feelings at the end of each day. A nice big journal that I can fill with letter after letter written to myself. As I'm planning this move and imagining what sort of notebook to buy, I think, 'Actually I can touch type really fast, so it would make more sense to type it up on the computer.' I imagine opening a Word document and hiding it in a file somewhere on the hard drive so that it's tucked away in a private place just for me. Then one thought turns to another and I think that if I'm going to type it on the computer I might as well use one of those blogging templates that are freely available online. No one need know I'm doing it. And if a random person in the world stumbles across it they won't know it's me, it can still be private and personal and just for me. I won't say who I am or offer any identifying details. It will be a personal journal for me, a private online diary to chart my progress.

I like making this plan. I like that I feel determined and focused. I don't particularly like that I feel quite alone in this monumental ambition but I can't see any other way forward. This really is just about me talking to me. Me fixing me.

My hangover fades and I get through the next two days in a low-key, glum state but with no alcohol passing my lips. Not-drinking hasn't been too difficult so far. I know I can live dry for periods at a time and I've just recently had three-and-a-half weeks entirely off the booze. It's just that this time the dry period will never end. That's how I'm going at this. I'm not thinking, 'Just for today I won't drink'; I'm thinking, 'I'm now a non-drinker.' It's a bit mind-boggling but that's my attitude. I'm expecting there to be a period of adjustment and I know that I'll have to be strong at times to resist urges but I'm determined that I'll be able to manage it. I'll just white-knuckle through the urges until the urges fade away and stop altogether. Surely they will. It's got to be that simple, right? Breaking a habit, that's what I'm doing. Removing alcohol and breaking a nasty little habit.

In these first few days I find myself doing unfamiliar things like buying energy drinks and iced coffees during the day and little bottles of soft drinks to pour in a wineglass at 5 p.m. (Well, why not? I don't want to suffer stem withdrawals.) I'm very focused on liquids. I'm not fighting any strong cravings but I'm also trying to head them off at the pass by having other drinks around me. And I go to the local library and grab all the books I can on drinking and living sober. I feel a little bit awkward at the front desk getting all these books on alcoholism but I tell myself that for all the librarian knows I could be doing my Master's research on alcohol (I'm not—it's on ethics in reality TV!). And anyway, I'm not an alcoholic, just a problem drinker.

By Thursday I have figured out how to set up a blog using the free service Blogger. It's incredibly easy to navigate around their site. I choose a URL that makes plain my goal—www.livingwithoutalcohol.blogspot.com—but the title of the blog I make more direct, more about me (although nice and enigmatic): *Mrs D Is Going Without*. I decide on a typeface (jaunty), a background (gritty), colours (bold) and I pinch a couple of images off the internet to liven up the page (feminine and boozy). It's my third day sober and I quickly write my first ever blog post to me. In it I tell the full story of my final night of drinking and express how I've had enough of this boozy madness. I'm honest and I'm direct. I'm talking to myself and I end it with a sign-off and kisses like I would any letter to a loved one, using my newly selected, enigmatic nom-de-plume.

Mrs D Is Going Without (Day 3)

I've reached a tipping point and from now have decided to remove alcohol from my life. I'm scared, it's going to be hard. Our family all drink. Our friends all drink. And I'm going to try and do this without any outside support. Just this blog. So stay posted and I'll let you know how I get on.

Love, Mrs D xxx

The act of setting up the blog, fiddling around with the template and making decisions about how it's going to look feels very satisfying, very active, like I'm doing something positive. I know that I'm going to have to retrain my brain to live without alcohol. I know that I've got a nasty habit to break and it will take some effort. Setting up the blog feels somehow like it's going to support me in that. And writing the first post feels great! I enjoy the process of telling the story, letting the words flow out of me. I type it out quickly then get on with the day knowing that the blog is there like a support net for me to fall back on.

Friday dawns and I wake up immediately thinking about my big decision and my exciting secret online journal. While the new sober lifestyle feels scary and overwhelming, the blog on the other hand feels treat-y, special and fun, like my own cool, online hideaway. I haven't told Corin about it yet, it feels too precious to share even with him. I hop online as soon as I can and read over my post from the day before. My own words on the screen stare back at me, spelling out the story of my last, sad evening of drinking. I launch straight into typing out a new post without too much planning.

Mrs D Is Going Without (Day 4)

Jeepers, reading that story in black and white does just the trick I hoped it would. It sure does read 'dysfunctional'. I think I might write out a couple more sad, unhealthy, dysfunctional facts about my drinking to ram this mission home. Because right now I'm thinking it's going to be a doddle to give up booze! But it's only been a few days and the memory of recent binges looms large in my brain. I'm sure as the weeks go by I'll be lulled into thinking I can start again, pressure will come on, and the pull, the incredible pull of the booze will call to me . . .

I fill out the rest of the post by confessing to some of my secret sick drinking habits (fixating on how much I can get in me, filling glasses to the rim and slurping the top down immediately, obsessing about how much others are drinking and how much is left for me). Some of the twisted drinking behaviours that have been my guilty secrets for so long come out of the dark corners of my mind, travel down my arms, into my fingers and through the keyboard to take shape on the screen. It feels *really* good to be getting it out. Empowering. Freeing. I close the post by looking at what's facing me for the night ahead.

Mrs D Is Going Without (Day 4 continued . . .)

Today is the opening of the Rugby World Cup and New Zealand is going nuts. We are heading down to the waterfront with the kids to soak up some of the Opening Party atmosphere then home to watch the All Blacks play the opening game. Usually I'd have a good bottle and a half of red wine to accompany that . . . but not tonight . . .

7

It is an incredibly unfortunate twist of timing. My new non-drinking life is beginning just as New Zealand is gearing up to host the Rugby World Cup. The event is being touted as 'The Biggest Party Ever!' and the entire country is going crazy with joy at celebrating such a huge, global event and of course (aside from the rugby) the whole thing seems to be about alcohol. Every alcohol company is sponsoring something to do with the event, every booze outlet is running special deals to aid with the partying, and the media is awash with suggestions on how to host game-day parties. Am I stupid? Am I mad to try and give up booze when there is such a noisy dialogue all around me about drinking, partying and having fun?

I can't afford to give a toss about the World Cup. I just can't. It could be Christmas, New Year or any other celebration and I'd still have to not-drink. I feel so determined to change my life, I'm not going to let anything stop me. I'm focusing only on what's inside my head: my own thoughts and my certain knowledge about my issues and the need for me to stop drinking. I'm not going to dwell or feel sorry for myself. I have to redefine myself as a non-drinker regardless of what is going on around me. I just have to forge ahead.

Corin and I brave the crowds and take the boys downtown to join in the opening night celebrations. We need to catch a train to the waterfront; there'll be no chance of parking the car in town. At the local station the platform is crowded and buzzing, our boys are excited and jumping about, and when we finally make it onto a train it's packed to the gunnels. Everyone is really excited and doesn't seem to mind that space is tight and the train is moving at a snail's pace. Thankfully the boys calm down in the crush and stand quietly holding tightly on to our hands.

At the front of our carriage is a group of pimply youths: they look nice enough but for one fact—they're absolutely trolleyed. It's 3 p.m. and they're drunk as skunks. I look at them from my safe distance at the other end of the carriage and feel not in the slightest bit jealous, but at the same time readily identifying with them—I've been there many a time.

As the train slowly inches towards town their drunken revelry gets louder until suddenly a chant builds up: 'Fill the bottle! Fill the bottle! Fill the bottle!' It takes me a while to register what they mean. Then the disgusting reality dawns on me. I look disbelievingly at Corin; surely they couldn't be encouraging their mate to piss in a bottle?

They are and, can you believe it, he does. He pisses in a bottle, holding it proudly aloft once he finishes—a 1-litre Coke bottle now filled with steaming yellow urine. I simply cannot believe this charming drunken act has happened right before my eyes just as I'm confronting my own drinking issues. My mind easily brings forward memories of being horribly drunk, an out-of-control feeling, a feeling of needing to piss, needing to vomit, needing to lie down, needing to stop. Watching this drunken behaviour from the other end of the carriage I have to admit that, right now, I feel great!

But my smugness is fleeting. Just a couple of hours later, having finally made it into town, we're pushing the pram along the waterfront through the crowd past a row of newly built bars and restaurants. The sun is streaming down and everyone is happy and friendly. Trendy parents with kids and mugs of beer sit on wooden benches with the sea lapping nearby. Young professionals laugh together, holding shiny glasses of chardonnay. And *bam!* I'm hit with a pang. A longing. An actual physical pain in my belly. And my inner dialogue, my drinking voice, starts up. 'Surely not. Never again? Really? Will I never again have that fun feeling, that freedom, that abandon? Will I never again experience that chatty, hedonistic, boozy fun?' I try to shut the voice up but there's no denying I feel glum. I feel shitty. I feel hard-done-by. The night ends with me on a bit of a downer.

The next morning I hop online and write a new post on my secret, private blog. I write out all that happened on our trip into town, the drunken youths, the piss in a bottle, the trendy bars and the pang. Once again I talk firmly to myself, referring to myself in the third person like a weirdo:

Mrs D Is Going Without (Day 5)

Remember Mrs D, remember.

It had stopped being fun.

It had stopped being fun.

It had stopped being fun.

But as the weekend progresses, I find myself completely freaking out. I manage to get through a quiet Saturday evening without drinking (early to bed) but wake up on Sunday morning in a total flap. A week hasn't even passed since I decided to become sober yet I've got a sick, uneasy, nervy feeling in my stomach. I'm far from relaxed. I'm worried. I haven't proven myself capable yet. I haven't had any serious temptations yet. What if I can't stay strong and never ever drink again? Can I actually do this?

Maybe one of the reasons I'm feeling so fraught is that I've been reading through my library books and they're all full of doom and gloom. They're all telling me that alcohol addiction is impossible to overcome, that willpower won't work, that I can't get sober alone, and that I'm going to remain miserable, with a perpetual longing forever more. I can't bear the thought.

On Sunday I secretly, desperately update my blog:

Mrs D Is Going Without (Day 6)

Okay, now I see why my guts are churning. I'm being told left, right and centre that I can't do this. Or at least that I can't do this alone.

But I'm not alone!!! I have you, dear blog. Dear Blog. Dearest Darling Blog. You are going to help save me. I will do it by writing you every morning. Together we can kick my booze-habit's butt. See you tomorrow.

Of course my blog is just me talking to me. It's a private journal that happens to be online. I'm relying on myself to keep myself sober. I like my secret forum where I can talk to myself and keep myself honest. It helps, but I'm still nervous as all hell about what I'm attempting to do. Determined, but nervous.

That evening I face a small social test. Corin's co-host and her husband invite us over for dinner. It's an easy way for me to test my newly acquired sober identity in a social setting but not a very tough one; these people don't know me at all. They offer us beer and wine on arrival and the 'not for me thanks' trips easily off my tongue. For all they know this is normal. Ha! Close friends would probably be checking my temperature right now and asking me if I wanted to lie down. I'm acutely aware of the alcohol around me and the others who are drinking it but it's not seriously tempting me. There's no noisy internal conversation within myself, trying to deny the urge, push it away, justify the want and then buckling to accept the wine.

It's not quiet in my mind, though—there's a raucous internal conversation going on about how pleased I am that I'm not drinking. I'm delighted with myself! I'm high-fiving myself mentally for being so strong! It's strange because my joy is monumental, yet it's hidden. I feel like I'm wearing a big furry gorilla suit that no one else can see. (I'm actually wearing a lovely pink tunic top which I have borrowed from my sister.)

The dinner progresses uneventfully and is mercifully brief. I'm sure no one at the table has any idea what's going on in my head; from the outside I appear quite calm. As we head home in the car, I'm on a bit of a high about how comfortable I felt not-drinking in that social setting. I rabbit on to Corin about what a great victory it was for me, but I don't think he quite understands how happy my behaviour tonight has made me. I'm so happy I don't even care when I get home and discover that I've been wearing my pink top inside-out the whole evening. The tag is totally showing at the back of my neck and all the seams are obviously on raggedy display. Big-time fashion fail. Oh well, whatever. I can't be bothered feeling embarrassed about that, I've got bigger stuff going on.

Sadly, my high doesn't last. The next day I wake up in grumpy-land, and as the week progresses I get more and more snippy by the day. I'm not seriously considering drinking but I feel grouchy as all hell. I thought I'd be feeling happier, lighter, free! I've got no hangovers, no guilt, and I'm sleeping right through every night (as opposed to my alcohol-induced insomnia). So why am I so tense? I snap at Corin all the time and yell at the kids for the slightest infringement. Jeez, I wish I could lighten up. I wish I could just shrug my shoulders and smooth myself out. I wish I was feeling great—I should be feeling great. Why aren't I feeling great?

One of my library books tells me that an alcoholic's brain adopts a peculiar amnesia, and as more time passes since the last drink they conveniently forget all of the reasons why they had to stop. I am *not* an alcoholic, that's a fact, but I can almost feel this peculiar amnesia happening inside my own brain. Thoughts fly in like: 'Do I really need to stop?' 'Is this drastic measure an overreaction?' 'Was I really that bad?' I have to work hard to not let myself forget the horrible boozy madness that I've been living. Yes, I bloody was that bad, I tell myself. Harrumph.

I update my secret blog every morning:

Mrs D Is Going Without (Day 8)

It's one week since my final binge, and I'm so aware that it's early, early days yet. But I haven't wanted a drink at all and don't feel nervous about any upcoming weekends or events. I feel like I never want to pour myself another glass of wine and go back down that track. But I'm nervous because I just know it can't be this easy.

Big deep breath in … whoosh … let breath out. In, out. In, out …

I'm working really hard inside my brain to try and change how I'm thinking. Because I'm going after this non-drinking as a long-term thing, I keep trying to visualise myself in the future—living completely sober. It's still a bit of a mind-fuck; picturing myself sober at all future events is horrendous. So I start shifting my thinking to a more short-term view, picturing myself getting through just the evening ahead without booze.

The evenings are bloody hard. Five o'clock might not be wine o'clock for me anymore but it still bloody happens every day.

As the clock inches closer to that crucial hour, of course I'm thinking about wine and start feeling uptight and glum that I can't have any. I try really hard to picture myself climbing into bed later on without having had anything to drink. I force myself to imagine getting into my PJs and brushing my teeth without having had anything to drink. It's fucking hard at 4.45 p.m., hard at 5 p.m. (pour a ginger beer into a wineglass), hard at 6 p.m. (grit my teeth and get on with the housewifey jobs), hard at 6.45 p.m. (pour another ginger beer), but by the time 7.30 p.m. rolls around the relief starts to creep in. I start to relax and breathe a bit easier and deeper. And, boy, it's lovely to actually follow through and find myself getting into bed every night without having had a drink. Really, really lovely.

Visualising myself sober in the long-term is much more painful and there's a bit to prepare for. My stepbrother's wedding is coming up. It's an Indian-themed event and every time I try to force my brain to imagine myself standing at the venue (in my sari) drinking something-not-wine, I get butterflies.

On top of that I've also got a huge event of my own around the corner—my 40th birthday. In just one month I'm turning the big Four-Oh and it's going to be a big party at a bar in town, combined with my brother-in-law who is also turning 40 at the same time. This party has been in the works for ages, and I've got loads of friends and family all set to come. Oh god. I try to picture myself sober at it, and it's not the greatest thought.

Me at my party trying to have fun while not-drinking. Everyone else drinking and having fun. Super.

It's such a bugger that the party is so soon. I'm sorry to say I wish it wasn't happening at all. But I don't know what I can do about it. I can't cancel out of a combined party. But I can't drink at it, either—no way. I'm just going to have to do the damn thing boring and sober and get through it.

All this thinking and planning and visualising is taking up a lot of brain time. Most of my waking hours are being spent thinking about me and alcohol and what I'm trying to do. I'm completely obsessed. I'm thinking about being sober as much as I used to think about drinking! There's a university lecture on sobriety permanently taking place in my brain. But it's strange and lonely because no one knows what I'm doing. No one even knew I had a problem and now they don't know what I'm doing to fix it. It's all crazily secretive.

At some point I'm going to have to tell people that I've made a big decision about my life and that it's taking an awful lot of work to implement. But I'm nervous as all hell about telling people. I don't want to make a twat of myself if I fail. And who just stops drinking? Who just ups and announces to the world that they have a hidden problem with alcohol and they're going to remove it completely?

But I do have a problem. And I do have a plan. And I do want to succeed. Which means at some point I'll have to come clean about what's going on.

8

The rest of Week Two is tricky. I'm constantly wrestling with my thoughts, going back and forth inside my mind about my decision not to drink. One minute I'm feeling good and strong about it, the next minute I'm doubting I was even that bad and wondering how the hell I'm going to never touch booze again. I'm floundering around with little information so in the evenings, instead of sitting on the sofa drinking wine and watching mind-numbing television, I sit on the sofa ordering library books about alcohol from the online catalogue. It's like I'm cramming for an exam on booze. And every morning I update my blog about what I'm doing and how I'm feeling.

The blog is actually having quite a considerable impact on my days. I'm finding that having my blog outlet makes it easier for me to venture out into my day. It's great knowing that I've got my private place to retreat back into to express myself. Putting everything into words helps me clarify how each new sober situation feels. Every morning I type up my experiences from the day before, and little reminders about how bad I was when I was still necking wine like it was going out of fashion. I dash off posts quickly then get on with my life, my own words lingering with me all day. When writing to myself I seem to be adopting an attitude that is upbeat and supportive, so the 'me' in print is buoying along the 'me' in the real world, which is nice.

I'm careful to only write about myself as much as possible, I'm aware that even though the blog is anonymous, it is available to the whole world! Even though I'm pretty sure no one would be interested even if they did come across my self-obsessed musings, I'm careful to keep it focused on me and the only aspect of my life I feel the need to write about—the not-drinking. My relationship with Corin, our kids and what they're doing, that's all private, and, frankly, irrelevant. In my situation the war is between my brain and alcohol, there's no one else involved with that. I want to keep the blog as focused as my thoughts are toward my problem. This is me fixing me.

It really is a godsend that I'm enjoying writing in my blog so much because the not-drinking largely sucks. Okay, so going to bed at night with no wine in my belly is glorious, as is sleeping right through the night and waking up clear-headed with no sick guts. But having to imagine myself sober at every social event in the future is hard. I'm really worried that I'm just going to be a boring, sad, sober loser for the rest of my life. My thoughts are bouncing around inside my mind like a frantic ping-pong game. I'm still determined but feel a little unsure of the likelihood that I can stick to my resolve.

I don't have to wait long before I'm tested socially again. Corin's parents are visiting from Christchurch and I take the boys over to my sister-in-law's place after school to see them. We're excited to catch up and soon after our arrival (at 3.30 p.m. it must be noted) my mother-in-law chimes up with 'I've got the wine chilling, would you like a glass?' Luckily for me my sister-in-law answers quickly with a 'Not for me thanks' and I follow swiftly with the same. I don't tell them about my big decision. It feels *so weird* to be saying 'no' and of course I'm nonstop in my mind thinking about it. Pre-monumental-life-changing-decision I'd be super-enthusiastic about having a wine, 'Yeah, go on!', but not today.

I spend the rest of the visit outwardly chatting and happy but inwardly obsessively thinking about how incredible it is that I'm not-drinking. When I bundle the boys in the car to drive home at around 5 p.m. it's amazing how proud of myself I am that I was able to resist. Another small victory!

Driving home I remember all the times I've had a social drink with someone in the afternoon only to find myself obsessing afterwards about whether to stop and buy more booze to continue drinking at home. Once I had a wine in me, all I wanted was more. I'd have a huge argument inside my mind about whether I should get more or not, and the 'Yes, drink more' voice would always win and see me detouring via the bottle shop. Today as I indicate to turn left into our street and *not* right to head to the bottle shop (yay!) I can remember how it feels to drink all that extra wine while getting the kids organised for bed. It doesn't feel light and fun. It feels boring, intense, determined, obsessed and unhealthy.

Tonight, instead of coming home on a boozy mission, I come home ridiculously elated at my non-drinking cleverness, once again high-fiving myself mentally. All I did was say no to a wine on a Thursday afternoon. You'd think I'd just won a prize or something! I'm so positive and my goal feels a little more possible. Oh happy non-drinker me.

Unfortunately, once again, this elation is short-lived. Despite my small not-drinking victory and yet another great night's sleep, the next day I find myself feeling all teary and weird. Talk about up and down, up and down, up and bloody down. I hate this. Corin comes home from work around lunchtime and I try to explain to him how I'm feeling and the bloody tears start falling out of my eyes before I've finished my first sentence. Tears. Falling out of my eyes. This is decidedly uncomfortable for me. This is not how I am. I don't like to be all teary and miserable. This is not me, I'm upbeat Lotta! But I can't stop crying.

I tell him that I feel raw and 'stripped back'. I flounder around trying to explain it: 'It's kind of . . . um . . . like . . . instead of my brain being under the influence of alcohol all the time . . . ah . . . I now have a brain that is sober all the time . . . and . . . um . . . it's just confronting, I suppose.'

He's lovely and kind but I feel a bit uncertain about what it is I'm actually trying to explain. I mean, it's not like my brain was under the influence of alcohol 24 hours a day, 7 days a week. I only drank after 5 p.m.(ish). So why at midday on a Friday would I be noticing that I feel raw and stripped back? I can't believe not-drinking is having this much impact on my overall emotional state. I can't believe I feel so different. Why? *Why?*

That night we head up the road to our friends' house for an early fish'n'chips dinner with the kids. Corin has a glass or two of red wine but the couple we're visiting rarely drink (they definitely don't have a problem) so it's pretty easy for me to abstain. I consider telling them about the big decision I've made but something stops me. I'm just feeling kind of weird and raw and low-key and self-protective. The night ends peacefully and I fall into bed exhausted. There's no celebration at having got through another alcohol-free night, just a sort of weary flatness.

But oh witness the delighted me waking up on Saturday morning with no hangover! It feels like Christmas! I'm upbeat again! I'm kind of in awe of myself as I make breakfast for the kids and carry a cup of tea to Corin in bed. Get me, oh clever, hangover-free me! I decide to forgo my usual instant coffee and instead make a green tea from a box that's been in the pantry for months. I put a bit of honey in it and feel a bit like a hippy but also really good. My nonstop internal dialogue is extremely self-satisfied. I appreciate the lack of a headache. I appreciate the settled stomach. I really appreciate the good night's sleep. I take deep breaths all morning and feel great as I move about the house.

Great, although still low-key, kind of nervous, and totally and utterly mentally obsessed with not-drinking.

The day progresses and my self-satisfaction fades away as we gear up to host Corin's parents for dinner. They arrive at 4.30 p.m. armed with beer and wine. Shitballs. They don't know about my decision yet. I haven't told anyone except Corin.

Everyone gets sorted with a drink. I have ginger beer and no one makes any comment. Maybe they don't even notice I'm not hooking into the wines like I used to? It seems strange to me that they wouldn't, given I feel like there's a giant neon sign above me flashing with the word 'SOBER!'

I slowly tense up as the evening progresses. I'm certainly not having the most fun time in the world and I'm aware that outwardly I'm being a bit grouchy. I feel bummed out that I can't just have a couple of drinks like everyone else (although they are all drinking very slowly, it must be said). Generally I just feel tense and grouchy and kind of flat and boring.

Corin sidles up to me in the kitchen at one point and quietly asks how I'm going. 'Okay,' I whisper. 'But I do feel quite uptight.' He gives me a quick cuddle and I feel better.

The night ends okay and as soon as I can in the morning I jump online to update my blog. I try to unpick what it was that was making me tense the night before:

Mrs D Is Going Without (Day 13)

I do feel more uptight on an evening like last night because:

1) I'm not relaxing with the alcohol in my system

2) I'm not part of the 'fun' group having a few drinks

3) I'm having to mentally process abstaining from something 'fun' so I'm concentrating on those serious thoughts = serious mood.

Hopefully 3) won't apply forever because I won't have to think about abstaining so much, I'll just automatically do it, and as for 2) readers of this blog will know (ha ha! That's a joke! I have no readers!) it wasn't fun anymore for me anyway.

Analysing in print why I was feeling tense last night is really helpful. And I enjoy making jokes with myself as well. I'm surprised to see the upbeat me coming through on the blog even though I'm grumpy. Nothing like a few exclamation marks to lighten my mood!!! I work hard to remind myself that if I'd been drinking last night I would have had at least five big glasses of wine (more like buckets really) while the in-laws were around and a couple more alone before I went to bed. It was a Saturday night after all and with family visiting I, no doubt, would have seen it as a good opportunity to drink heavily.

Later that day I head off to the mall on my own to do some shopping. I bump into some friends in the food hall and, without really planning it, I blurt out my news. 'So I've given up drinking,' I breezily announce with chopsticks in hand, 'like, forever.'

They seem quite taken aback. Interested but not saying much.

'I'm just sick of not controlling it,' I say, 'so I'm taking it away completely.'

They act a bit bemused. 'Are you really that bad?' one friend asks.

'Yep,' I say, firmly stabbing at a dumpling, 'I am.'

I know I'm laying myself on the line here, but I cling to the truth that only I (and the non-existent readers of my secret blog) know how big a problem I really have.

Mrs D Is Going Without (Day 14)

It's hard for people to really get it. No one really knows except you, the drinker.

No one else can hear your inner voice and feel your insane pull to drink.

No one else knows your sneaky filling of each glass to the rim and slurping the top down immediately.

No one else knows your one or two drinks out with friends will end in a trip to the store on the way home for another bottle to finish up because once you've started it's very very very very hard to stop.

I head into my third sober week pleased that I managed to get through a busy social weekend without too much trouble. Corin has to travel away for work for a few days so it's just the boys and me back in our weekly routine. I keep buying myself energy drinks and iced coffees during the day, and pouring myself soft drinks in a wineglass on the dot of 5 p.m. There is some wine leftover in the fridge from the weekend but I don't touch it. My internal dialogue is still just as noisy and busy, though, and I spend a lot of time thinking about how nice it is to be not boozing and worrying constantly like I used to. I write a blog post most days and feel oh so very clever and sober.

I start to relax and think maybe, just maybe, it is going to be this easy.

Then *bam!* Thursday hits and it's a shitter. A complete shitter of a day. It starts at 5 a.m. with our youngest boy waking up and refusing to go back to sleep. Five a.m. is the middle of the bloody night as far as I'm concerned. Not happy. Not happy at all. Then our eldest pesters and pesters and pesters me to help with some stupid computer game before school, which I do not have the time or patience for, and, oh boy, do I yell at him. I yell and yell and yell. Then after the school drop-off I go to Warehouse Stationery and discover at the counter that my money cards are not in my bloody wallet. Fucking kids!

I come home extremely grumpy and now the house is my enemy, it feels really dusty and gross and I just feel really shitty and tired and frankly pissed off that I can't buy any wine to drink tonight. Maybe I should just buy a fucking bottle and drink it? Maybe I don't even need to stop? Maybe I wasn't that bad after all?

I'm not sure what to do with myself so I go online. This is the first time I have written a post in the middle of the day, in the middle of a sober crisis.

Mrs D Is Going Without (Day 17)

I'm really tired and really shitty and really would love a drink. There, I said it.

Usually I'd drink a bottle (and a bit) of wine at the end of a day like this and then sleep like crap and then feel even tireder tomorrow. So the wine doesn't make me rested. Does the wine help relieve any stress? No. Is the wine fun and naughty and does it take me away from my hard boring life as a housewife and mother of three? Yes!! Yes, yes, yes it does.

Don't worry, I'm not going to drink. No way. I just have to live this shitty grumpy tired day and go to sleep tonight and maybe tomorrow will be easier.

Okay, a plan: 40 minutes of hard-out cleaning to make me feel better about the house and then I can sit down to relax until Little Guy wakes up from his nap.

I'm sure no one is reading my blog but me so the 'Don't worry, I'm not going to drink' is aimed at myself. That feels good. I finish the post, put my yellow rubber gloves on and clean. I clean and scrub and clean and scrub and as 5 p.m. approaches I work hard to picture myself getting into bed sober. I manage to get through and feel really happy and proud when I finally hit the hay at 8.30 p.m . . . But I am a bit shaken at how difficult it was to get through that grumpy shitty day without turning to my beloved wine at 5 o'clock. I decide to increase the pressure on myself to stick to my resolve by telling more people about what I am doing.

I start with my big sister down the phone line. It just comes out because when we're talking about something unrelated, I start crying. It's definitely an overreaction to the topic at hand and not usual behaviour from me so I feel the need to explain myself: '(sob sob) . . . the reason . . . (sniff) . . . that I'm crying is that actually . . . (sniff sniff) . . . I've

decided to give up alcohol completely and it's just making . . .
(sob) . . . me feel . . . (sniff sniff) . . . quite raw and emotional
. . . I guess.'

She's taken aback. 'Really? Why?'

And I truthfully reply that I've been drinking an awful
lot and was finding it very difficult to control.

She hears what I'm saying and gives me some lovely
encouragement. 'Man you're awesome, you're so incredibly
strong, that is amazing,' which makes me feel good.

I decide it's time to let my parents know what I'm up to.
They both live in Christchurch (where I grew up), but are
divorced and in separate houses with new partners now, so
a phone call to each is the only way. I ring my dad first; he's
quietly supportive and impressed. Then I ring my mum. She's
definitely surprised but is supportive as well. I'm shaking
through both phone calls—it's such an intense process, I'm
really laying myself on the line here.

Now that I've started telling people there's no stopping
me. I go to pick up one of the boys from a birthday party and
the host mum offers me some bubbles (there are a few other
mums there already drinking, sigh). She raises her eyebrows at
me when I turn her down so I tell her I've stopped drinking,
point at the glass and say in a faux chirpy way, 'The thing is
I don't just want one of those, I want six!' She's a bit taken
aback but pours me a Coke in the champagne flute instead
and I awkwardly sip at it. I feel self-conscious and odd. But

time passes and something really cool happens. I get chatting to the other mums and forget momentarily that my glass doesn't contain alcohol. I relax a bit. And I chat. And it's okay. My face doesn't fall off and nobody storms away from me in a huff. I just stand and chat and drink my Coke and it's fine. Another small victory! High-fives all round! (Well, in my mind anyway.)

Next day I tell my sister-in-law when she's here having coffee and she confronts me with a shocked, 'What?! Never again?!'

I try to sound confident. 'Um, yeah, that's the plan,' I say with a gulp. 'I mean, life is really long, but, yeah, that's the plan.' Then I fling my arms open and loudly declare, 'Say Hello To The New Sober Lotta!' (Never forgo the opportunity for a dramatic moment, right?)

Announcing my plan to people is empowering yet kind of intimidating. Basically what I'm doing is outing myself as a problem drinker. I mean, normal drinkers don't give up alcohol, do they? It's refreshing in some ways—a relief to be brutally honest to everyone about my secret dysfunction. But at the same time it's really scary as I'm setting myself up to be watched now.

But I press on and continue to lurch through the days feeling elated, self-satisfied, nervous, grumpy, teary or all of the above inside a single hour. I'm confused about why I'm all over the show emotionally and my internal dialogue about alcohol, drinking, not-drinking still fiercely rages on. I write regular posts on my blog and keep coming up with bad drinking memories that I type out determinedly. I don't drink (shit fuck bloody fucking not-drinking shit) but I eat lots and lots, come down with a bad head cold and get a big pimple on my chin. A pimple! A great big red angry pimple! I haven't had a pimple for years. What the hell is happening to my body? To my mind?

I feel mixed up, unsettled, and so completely different to what I'm used to feeling and how I like to exist that subsequently I'm quite at odds with myself.

Then sitting on the sofa one evening, eating too many biscuits and watching *The Oprah Show*, a bombshell drops. Yes, that's right. Oprah delivers me a monumental 'Aha!' moment. How clichéd is that?

9

The show is about chronically overweight people—compulsive overeaters. She's got a couple of them on the stage opening up about their personal struggles and in the front row of the audience are some experts to offer sage advice. One of these experts, a doctor I think he is, starts talking about how emotionally disturbed people might try to control their emotions by overeating or doing drugs or drinking heavily. Oprah-the-Wise then says, 'All of those habits are just different ways to squash down emotions, aren't they?'

My brain does a small explosion. I kid you not. It is like a bomb goes off in my mind. Sitting on the sofa, I pause the TV, put my hand up to cover my mouth and freeze. I'm not being overly dramatic here, this is actually what I do. I freeze, with my hand over my mouth, staring off into wide open space, and a realisation starts to dawn on me. For the first time in a long time it's quiet in my mind and I struggle to form my thoughts. 'Have I . . . is my . . . . . . has my wine drinking . . . has it been . . . emotional . . . my steady constant wine drinking . . . am I . . . do I want to squash . . . is that what I've been doing?'

Is *that* why I'm such a wreck right now?

Here I am, an intelligent, well-read, mature woman who likes to think of herself as being in tune with people and wise in the ways of the world, yet I feel utterly stunned by this revelation. I don't even know if this is a revelation. It's a small brain explosion at any rate. Is it possible that, unbeknown to me, I have been drinking to avoid being emotional? I thought I was a party girl who drank to have fun. I thought my heavy drinking of late was just that my habit had gone too far. I thought what I was doing in stopping drinking was just breaking a habit. I think that's what I thought. I don't know what to think. This is unexpected.

Mrs D Is Going Without (Day 22)

I ate a lot yesterday. Pigged out. Then in the evening I was watching Oprah recorded from earlier in the day and she had a doctor talking about how emotionally disturbed people might control their emotions and one way was drugs and alcohol addiction, another was overeating. She said people eat a lot to 'squash down their emotions'. So, have I been using alcohol to squash down emotions and yesterday did I overeat to squash down the emotions I'm feeling about my big life change?

Interesting.

Holy shit. If I've been using alcohol all this time to squash my emotions, do I now have to learn how to be emotional? I thought I was just learning how to not-drink.

The air around me has suddenly changed. I feel like I'm moving slower. I'm no longer just dealing unquestionably with the fact that I drink far too much and how to stop that, I'm now asking myself, 'Why?' Why have I been drinking heavily for years and years?

I start thinking back over my life. I try to remember my childhood. I get my old diary out from when I was a teenager and re-read it, along with letters I have received throughout the years and old notes to myself. The dusty pages contain a lot of angst and introspection—I certainly wasn't cool and calm in my earlier years. Reading it back now, it seems clear that I had no idea what kind of person I was, or what I should be doing to make myself feel happy. I spent a lot of time floundering around trying to figure out who I was and how I fitted in: moving around different groups of friends, moving to different high schools, moving to different cities and countries, moving, moving all the time. No terrible dramas, just a lot of moving around and searching for what feels right. Searching for fun and feeling good.

It think back over old friends and workmates from years gone by (I even try to find some of them with Google and on Facebook). I mentally retrace my steps after I left home and trawl through the story of my life so far; all the jobs I've had (mostly journalism and media related), houses I've lived in (flats with friends, homes of relatives), people I've known (so many lovely people coming in and out of my life constantly), places I've lived in (Christchurch, Sydney, Wellington, Christchurch, Wellington, London, Wellington, Auckland, Wellington), and all the many places I've travelled to.

I rake through the memories searching for some big answer as to why I'm a boozer. It's not an entirely comfortable process. It feels very 'navel-gazey' and I've always been very scornful about people who navel-gaze. I'm not one of those introspective soul-searchers, no way! I'm low-maintenance, fun, cruisey, upbeat Lotta, remember?

I find a lot of stuff, but I don't find a silver bullet. It's just a steady stream of average-life shit, a life filled with the normal (I assume) highs and lows; teenage angst and hopes and dreams, family fun and family dramas, bad relationships and good ones, supportive friends and destructive ones, insecurities and successes, knock-backs and triumphs, grief and joy, pain and laughter. Life stuff.

But all this moving and searching, and everywhere booze.

Lots and lots of drinking. Booze my steady companion from aged fifteen until three weeks ago.

I'm quite wiped out by this introspective process. None of this is coming easily and I haven't exactly leapt to a comfortable new understanding about myself. I'm not used to this sort of soul-searching. I'm not even sure if I'm searching my soul or just searching my memory bank. I don't know what the hell I'm doing. The only thing I do know is that I'm trying really hard to not drink anymore.

I do feel like I've taken a big step but I'm not quite sure in what direction. My mind is a whirling mass of contradictory thoughts and god I'm just sick and tired and raw and goddamn sober all the bloody time. *Aaarrrggghhh!!!* A glass of wine would be such a wonderful relief right now!

Then life happens. Our one-year-old—laughing wildly being chased by his big brother—trips and crashes into the door frame, splitting his head wide open.

Mrs D Is Going Without (Day 27)

Was pretty bloody knackered yesterday after spending all of Friday night in A&E with the Little Guy who fell on the door frame and split his head open. It happened at 6 p.m. and usually—pre-major-life-change to give up wine drinking—I would have had at least half a bottle in me by that point. But the new sober Mrs D was clear-headed enough to dial emergency and get an ambulance that took us to the hospital to get patched up.

Corin gets home from a long lunch just as the ambulance arrives. He stays home with the big boys while I go to hospital to get our little fella patched up. The head gets glued back together (not that bad in the end but there was a lot of blood) and of course it takes five hours at the hospital so on Saturday I'm beyond tired. I'm exhausted and grouchy and sensitive and *sober* yet again. I manage to drag myself through the day until about 5 p.m., when Corin (sitting comfortably on the sofa with a casual glass of red) says to me (standing at the dining table folding a huge pile of washing), 'It's going to be hard for you not to be able to have a release at the end of the day with a glass of wine anymore.'

This I don't need right now. I snap.

'But I don't just have one or two glasses of wine!' I hiss through gritted teeth while furiously balling socks. 'I have a bottle and a half! That fantasy of *just a couple to unwind* doesn't exist for me anymore.' This is not cruisey behaviour but I don't care.

Corin is a bit taken aback and tries to clarify his point. 'I just mean . . . um . . . it's going to take an adjustment . . . to not have that release because . . . um . . . that's how many of us use alcohol and . . .'

He's floundering around, poor guy, but I'm not in the mood to feel kindly about his attempts to understand what the hell I'm going through. It's not on! I'm the bloody expert on this! Sensitive much? I get grouchier and fiercely remind him about my determined overdrinking. 'The last thing I need is someone, especially you, working to undermine my resolve and lead me down the path of romantic reminiscing about drinking. I can't afford right now to think romantically about unwinding with a drink!' Romance be damned, my drinking was anything but romantic and my unwinding at the end of the day was more like a complete unravelling.

Is this a fight? We never fight. I hate fights. But I'm fired up. And I'm completely drained; physically and emotionally exhausted. I stomp around the house delivering piles of washing to various bedrooms, slamming drawers as I go. I feel shaky and teary and angry and fraught. Deep down I'm still determined not to drink but this is so hard! Much harder than I thought it was going to be. I didn't realise stopping drinking was going to be so goddamn *emotional* and confusing and hard to explain. I still feel incredibly alone in my thoughts. Am I the only one who understands what I'm going through?

I retreat into the kitchen and force myself to breathe slowly and deeply. I try really hard to slow my thoughts down and look at what's really wrong here. I'm ultra-tired and Corin's being a bit insensitive, I tell myself. But he doesn't mean to be.

He's trying to be truly supportive but the bottom line is, he doesn't really get what I'm going through. He can't get it. His brain is wired differently when it comes to booze. He can't hear my nonstop, anxious, confused and jumbled thoughts about drinking. I pour myself a glass of ginger beer then get busy whipping cream for pudding and put clean sheets on our bed. I think hard about getting into bed later with no wine in me. I am not having wine, I tell myself repeatedly.

We eat pudding (I have lots), but I'm still snippy so Corin offers to put the boys to bed so I can have a bath. He doesn't have to offer twice. I run a very deep bath filled with bubbles and as bedtime chaos rages down the hallway ('I want five books, Dad, not two!') I climb in to soak the tension away. Then I get into our freshly made bed. I am sober, I tell myself. I am not drinking wine. I am very clever and brave and sober.

This positive talk offers a tiny measure of comfort but doesn't remove the general uncomfortable feeling I have at being so grouchy and emotional, but I keep telling myself I have no choice. I have to keep going and learn how to do this. I will learn. Surely I will learn, eventually.

After Corin has managed to settle the boys he comes to the bedroom armed with white chocolate to sweeten me up. It works, the tension eases and he climbs in next to me to watch a World Cup match on the bedroom telly. I plug the laptop in and start searching around the internet for information about drinking (obsessed much?). I put headphones on and watch some YouTube clips of drunk people falling over, then some clips of addiction experts offering advice on how to quit drinking. I find a clip of a coach-type woman talking about how visualising yourself sober in the future can be really helpful. Hey—that's what I've been doing in my evenings! It's great to hear someone articulate this as a sobriety technique and I feel very clever for doing it myself.

Then I get an idea and type 'Sober Blogs' into Google and up pop a few—this is exciting! I find one called *Crying Out Now: Voices of addiction and recovery* which is full of stories submitted by women about their drinking problems. I read a bunch of these stories and it's comforting to see so many similarities to mine. I click around a bit more then come across a site called *Mr SponsorPants: An AA Sponsor Blog*. It's a cheerful-looking site, all orange and yellow with cute cartoon images of a white-haired dude all over it. As I read through some of his posts I deduce that whoever this guy is, he's been sober a long time and is full of great wisdom. Every post is brief and helpful, and illustrated with quirky images and motivational quotes.

Sitting in my bed with headphones on and the rugby playing in the background, I feel quite touched by what Mr SponsorPants is offering and suddenly decide to get brave and leave a comment. It feels so scary! But what the hell have I got to lose? No one can see who I am; I'm safely hidden behind my laptop, in my bed, in my house, down in my little corner of the world. I figure I'm invisible but for the words I leave at the bottom of his latest post:

Comment from Mrs D:

Hey just wanted to say thanks. I find your posts really useful. I am 1 month sober and going it alone aside from searching out people like yourself who share online. Plus I have a secret weapon blog I am hoping will help me stay strong. Cheers from NZ.

My hands are shaking as I copy and paste the URL from my blog into his comments section. What am I doing? I haven't even told Corin yet about my blog but here I am sending it out into the world. But I feel safe knowing that I'm anonymous. Mrs D could be anyone. No one can discover that I'm really Lotta Dann, wobbly, emotional mother-of-three trying desperately to not be a boozer in her suburban Auckland home. Surely it's got to be safe for me to push my blog out there into this online environment? I'm sick of feeling so alone, and Mr SponsorPants seems nice. What's the worst that can happen? Nothing, I decide and with shaking hands click 'publish'. I close the laptop and snuggle down to sleep.

First thing in the morning I hop back online and navigate to the Mr SponsorPants page. He has written a new post since I've been asleep! And I can't quite believe it, but it feels like he has written it just for me.

Post from Mr SponsorPants:

if you are new to sobriety

hold on

one day at a time.

there are not the words

for the transformation you can experience

I cry. I actually sit in my bed and I cry. It's like Mr SponsorPants has just kindly stroked the big knot of emotion and angst and fear and uncertainty in my belly and it's caused me to cry. It's a really bloody intense feeling.

After a few teary moments I wipe my eyes and click over to my own blog and open up a new post. I type out the discussion that Corin and I had the evening before, how angry I felt, how wound up I got, and how I calmed myself down. Then I determinedly type yet more reminders about why I am putting myself through this hell.

Mrs D Is Going Without (Day 28)

I don't miss going to the loo and looking at the back of the door thinking, 'I'm pissed'.

I don't miss going to the loo 3 times overnight.

I don't miss being awake in the wee small hours feeling guilty about how much wine I sank the night before.

I don't miss cursing that we have no Panadol in the house in the morning.

I don't miss yelling at the boys to stop yelling because my head is pounding.

I don't miss my guts churning and my head aching until mid-afternoon.

I don't miss dragging my sorry ass through the day because of a hangover.

I don't miss the sly fox in my brain thinking about how much wine to get, how much wine is left . . .

I don't miss that sly wine-drinking boozy fox at all.

Despite my fighting talk and the nice feelings my Mr SponsorPants experience has given me, the next week is a shitty one. I get drinking pangs, lots of them. I feel stuck in the thick mud of just trying to get through each day without drinking. I'm not exactly having a light and fun time of it. My stupid brain keeps pulling forward romantic images of alcohol; a nice cold chardonnay at the end of a long summer's day, a warming merlot on a winter's evening, bubbles to celebrate, whiskey to bond. And everywhere I look—on TV, in the newspapers, around the neighbour-hood—there's alcohol. I feel overwhelmed knowing that alcohol is everywhere, wedded into every aspect of our culture, soaking every corner of our world, and thinking that for the rest of my life I'm going to have to sit outside of that. It just feels so unfair! Am I the only boring, sober loser in the world? I do not like this new me. I do not like this new reality I have chosen for myself. I do not like this at all!

But I press on. I've got a dogged determination and I cling to the knowledge that I just *have to do this*. So I deal with the pangs when they come, fending them off one after the other, stubbornly refusing to buckle and drink again, desperately remembering why I stopped. I'm proud of myself that I'm not buckling and drinking, but also nervous and uncertain about what lies ahead and just so goddamn emotional all the time.

Mrs D Is Going Without (Day 31)

I just feel so scared. I've been pouring red wine down my throat like it's going out of fashion for years. For ages I've had an internal clock chiming a call to DRINK! At 5 p.m. I've got a brain that has spent hours and hours and hours affected by alcohol. Drinking it, recovering from it, feeling guilty about it, obtaining it, looking forward to it, drinking it, and so on and so on.

So why is my brain now just happily accepting my final decision to cut it out altogether? I'm fearful it's tricking me, lulling me into a false sense of security. I like to think I'm strong-minded and clear-headed and have never kidded myself about my dysfunctional unhealthy relationship with alcohol. But to have this decision to live sober be so easy . . . well, I'm scared.

Must remember, must remember, must remember.

My mood doesn't lighten as the week progresses and I stare down yet another non-drinking Friday night. My pimple is still there and I feel fat and unhealthy and miserable. On Friday morning I drag myself to the gym and sit on a bike for about 30 minutes doing what could best be described as a lacklustre workout. I'm so pissed off that I'm feeling so awful. Shouldn't I be riding a great wave of hangover-free joy? En route home I stop at the store and attempt to cheer myself up by buying a bunch of flowers and some yummy nibbles for the evening ahead—I figure that since I'm not bloody spending a hundred bucks (or more) on booze each week, I should treat myself a little. I get pistachio nuts and hummus and corn chips and some nice cheese. At the last minute I decide to be kind and buy Corin an expensive bottle of red wine. I'm not drinking, but why shouldn't he? It clinks in the bag as I put it in the car.

Was I really that bad?

When I get home I head to the computer to see if any new emails have come in. There's one. It's from Blogger. Why are they emailing me? Then I look closer and see that the subject line reads: 'You have a new comment.'

10

I get ridiculously excited. A comment! A comment for me! My heart is beating really fast as I click through to my blog. The comment has been left on the post I wrote almost a week ago about the heated discussion Corin and I had.

Comment from 'She'

Our husbands sound similar. They don't mean harm. Mine doesn't really know what it feels like to have a drink at 8 in the morning because you just can't not drink. It took him a while to get that his wife was a raging, shaking alky.

Keep going, we can do this for ourselves.

Whoa. This is so cool on so many levels. First of all, I'm just so chuffed that someone has written a comment to me. I read and re-read it about five times. It feels like this 'She' has reached from far away through the internet into my living room and given me a big hug—it is that tangible, the warmth I feel at reading what she wrote to me.

I dig the fact that She's in the same boat as me with a nasty drinking problem. I dig the fact that She, like me, has a husband that doesn't fully understand what it's like for us problem-drinkers. I dig the fact that She is being kind to me and I totally dig that She is buoying me along with her 'keep going, we can do this for ourselves'. I have support!

I click on the link attached to the 'She' name and it takes me through to a blog that She writes—and what do you know? It's an anonymous blog about trying to stop drinking! I read her latest post and write a comment in return—something encouraging and kind. Man, it feels good.

This online interaction totally transforms my day. I move through the rest of Friday feeling so much lighter and don't mind at all not having a glass of the expensive red I bought with Corin in the evening. I think about 'She', my commenter, and for the first time since I embarked on my new lifestyle I don't feel quite so alone.

Saturday morning dawns and I hop online as soon as I can to write a new post. My private blog now seems even more treat-y and special and I feel a surge of strength and determination. I write about 'She':

Mrs D Is Going Without (Day 33)

She is somewhere in America, trying, trying, trying, to become sober. She is a mother, a wife, a daughter and a drinker. I have posted comments to her blog, wishing her all the best, willing her to stay strong, willing her to victory over this nasty sly addiction. How crazy is it that this drug is so socially acceptable even though so many people struggle with it and it ruins their lives? I am determined to be one of those really cool, strong people who in years to come will say casually, 'Yeah, I gave up alcohol a while ago, it just wasn't agreeing with me anymore. I'm much happier without it in my life.'

That will be me.

That will be She.

I feel so great after writing this, because now I'm not only supported but *supportive*. It's a double whammy of support! For the first time since I hit my rock bottom (hiding the bottle) and decided to try and never drink again, I'm looking outward and not in. My viewpoint has momentarily shifted away from my own issues—nerves, grumpiness, pimples—to other people. It's so nice to be taken out of myself for a bit. I feel like I'm beating a little drum in my little corner of the world and it's faintly being heard elsewhere. Boy, does that make me feel good. I'm floating through Saturday when—can you believe it?!—I get more emails from Blogger, not one but *two* more comments arrive!

Comment from 'Anonymous'

Hello Mrs D. I had 5 months sober and loved it but recently I've slipped back into my old habits. I've read all of your posts and can see so much of my own story in your story. I'll be popping in to read your updates and wish you all the best. I want to be where you are now again. I felt so good when I didn't drink. I need to get that feeling back. Take care.

Comment from 'Nan'

Hi Mrs D, I just read your whole entire blog! So you see someone is reading! I find what you write about so honest and real. I've enjoyed reading and I'll be back!

They're talking to me. Talking. To. Me. Saying hello Mrs D, take care Mrs D. Wow! It's crazy just how much these comments mean to me. Two more big internet hugs. I'm even more buoyed along. I can feel a big resurgence of determination inside me. I can do this!

Another non-drinking Saturday night passes okay—I pour myself a ginger beer at 5 o'clock and push my thinking forward to bedtime to get myself through the witching hours without drinking. I know that I need to capitalise on this positive feeling. I know I've still got a lot of brain retraining to do. Sunday morning I wake up and can't wait to jump online and write a new post.

Mrs D Is Going Without (Day 34)

Okay, so now I'm thinking of some more of these casual statements that I'll trot out at social occasions in the years to come. This is a technique! Visualising myself sober. Projecting forth into the future a vision of a smart, cool and together Mrs D. Not the sloppy, lush-like ageing party girl that I had become.

So here goes.

At a wedding: 'Oh no, just a juice for me, thanks. Why? Oh, I just don't bother with the booze anymore, it was running away with me (tosses hair), but I'm no less fun, am I?' (Laughs gaily and spends the rest of the night cutting it up stylishly on the dance floor before driving all the drunk people home.)

At a work function: 'This? (points to glass) Oh, it's just tonic water, I'm not bothering with the hard stuff anymore. Trust me, I'm way better without it.' (Proceeds to spend the night talking wittily and intelligently with management, taking care of the new girl who overdoes it on chardonnay; drives home and reads two chapters of great novel before sleeping soundly all night.)

On a group holiday: 'No, really, I'm just having a Red

Bull. It's okay, really. No, it's not that hard (lies), I just don't want the alcohol in my life anymore. No, I'm not judging any of you guys, honestly, you just go for it.' (Retreats to bedroom to re-read letter written to self on first day of sobriety to remember, remember, remember why this must be done.)

It's fun writing this post and trying to make myself appear happy in these visions, but in reality I don't feel happy about it at all. In fact, I feel utterly glum. Can anything ever be fun again? I'd like to think I could be that hair-flicking, totally-fine-with-it, sparkly non-drinker but I just can't imagine it happening. Being clever, online Mrs D is great, but I know that I have to keep walking away from my computer and be sober Lotta dealing with reality. I have to actually go to actual real events in person and actually not-drink. Ever. Frankly, it's still bloody awful to contemplate. Boring, sad, sober and just not fun at all. I'm missing my old self, the fun up-for-it party girl.

I feel really depressed about it, actually. I've still got so much to get through. I'm kind of getting used to doing ordinary evenings at home without my beloved wine, but outside of home I've hardly had any tests. Just a couple of quiet meals with a few friends without much boozing going on by anyone involved. I haven't been to a rowdy dinner party or noisy bar. I haven't sat in the sun at a lush afternoon barbecue or gathered in a pub to celebrate something with mates. I haven't been to a glitzy function or indulged in a long lunch. I haven't been to a party, or a wedding.

Weddings. Don't talk to me about bloody weddings; we've got three coming up—*three!* And the first is just a couple of weeks away. It seems silly but I'm really nervous about having to go to these sober. What is a wedding if it's not a chance to partake of all the free booze? Okay, so there's also witnessing beautiful love, soaking up the lovely atmosphere and decorations, pigging out on yummy food and boogieing the night away to cheesy tunes. But I, for one, can't imagine enjoying any of that without loads of bubbles in me (no surprises there). Who goes to a wedding and doesn't drink heaps?

Comment from 'Nate'

I am going to a wedding in February and they have invited me despite knowing I am a wobbling drunk towards the beginning of the night. Will be refreshing to be there without drinking a single drop and being the driver.

First time for everything.

Ah, of course. Other reformed boozers don't drink at weddings. This chap (I check his login and, sure enough, another anonymous sober blogger!) offers me some comfort.

I'll think of him at the upcoming weddings. But first I've got a different bloody hurdle to get through—my 40th.

Turning 40 feels monumental, like I'm heading into a new phase in my life. It's probably no coincidence that I've chosen this time to undergo a monumental lifestyle change. On the night of my actual birthday Corin and I are going out for a fancy meal, and then a week or so later I've got the combined party with my brother-in-law. And in between those events I've got my stepbrother's wedding to go to and a big black-tie dinner to attend. It's awful to say but the whole lot feels like a giant ordeal because I have to not-drink through all of it. There's a big part of me that just wants to click my fingers and pop forward into the future to when it's all done and dusted.

But I can't do that. I have to step one sober foot in front of the other and get through everything. I have to do the lush birthday dinner not-drinking, go to the wedding not-drinking, then co-host a big party not-drinking. Fuck, what am I doing to myself? I'm feeling a huge weight of social pressure bearing down on me. I keep going back over my blog re-reading all the reasons I've typed out as to why I've stopped drinking. I'm forcing myself to remember very clearly that horrible boozy hell that I was living. I keep telling myself that this can be done. I can do it. I can. Can I?

The pressure does nearly undo me, but it's not during

any of the social events, but rather a random night at home in the midst of them all.

Mrs D Is Going Without (Day 41)

Had my 40th dinner out, a lovely long posh meal at a very expensive restaurant (will never do that again but it was a real treat) with Mr D. Started with tasty fruit cocktail and then sipped sparkling soda water for the rest of the meal. Mr D had 3 glasses of expensive wine, I even sniffed each one to get a sense of their beauty. Oh get me ... drinking problem? What drinking problem?!

That was Thursday night. Friday afternoon at the mall little thoughts started creeping in: 'Nothing to look forward to tonight *sigh*' and 'Boring, flat night ahead' and 'Why can't I have a bloody glass of wine'.

Pushed them aside, squashed them down, got through and went to bed at 8.30 p.m.

Then yesterday, Saturday, even stronger, jumbled together, a wave of thoughts: 'I would love a glass of wine it's not fair why can't I drink one it's Saturday night I should be able to have a drink everyone else is having a drink and having fun am I really not going to have a drink again ever my whole life why am I doing this again I should be able to have a drink what harm would it do the whole world drinks alcohol was I ever really that bad I could probably moderate I'm sure I'll be able to moderate now it's only wine it's not heroin I was never that bad no drunk-driving close relationships all functional didn't lose jobs or friends because of drinking so is wine really that bad it's Saturday night for god's sake everyone has a drink on Saturday am I the only sad sack in the world why am I doing this again I wasn't that bad was I it's not fair oh my god.'

Shut the fuck up. Shut. The. Fuck. Up.

I'm screaming at myself inside my own brain. The war is on and I am screaming. This wave of thoughts is like a bloody jackhammer hammering away at my brain. Hammering away at my resolve. Hammering away at my soul. Forgive me the drama but this really is such an overwhelming intense drinking pang. It's the pang to beat all pangs. I'm totally at war with my thoughts right now, my own brain is turning on me like a two-faced shitty friend. It would be so easy to just have a wine to shut up the voice in my head. Instead I inwardly scream.

Shut the fuck up goddamn it!!! Piss off!!!

Where the hell is this incessant thinking about alcohol coming from? Is it the wine talking? Is it the addicted part of my brain? Is it the naughty teenager in me that never grew up? Is it some sort of depressed person that I've never known was there?

Why is my Saturday night boring without alcohol? Why do I care so much about goddamn motherfucking alcohol?

I can't cope with this voice inside my brain telling me to drink. It will not stop. I feel like I'm losing control. It is so hard to fight this wave of thoughts leading me in the direction of a big fat glass of wine. I don't know what to do.

11

I can't let this fucking voice win. I have to get it out, get it out of my head and into the room, so I start talking about it, out loud to Corin. 'There's this voice inside my head telling me to drink,' I confess. 'It won't shut up. I'm obsessed. It's telling me I deserve to drink and I should just have a drink. It's telling me everyone else in the world is having a drink right now and I should just have one too. It's telling me I was never that bad and that it's not fair that I can't drink. It won't shut up. I want it to stop but it won't.'

Corin listens kindly as he always does and offers me some supportive comments, but I'm mad as hell and really wound up. I have to shut this fucking voice up. *I am not going to drink!*

So I keep talking out loud, babbling even, desperately, brutally honest: 'The thing is I don't just want one or two wines I want eight. And if I have any I'll sleep like crap and I'll wake up feeling like shit. I'll have a hangover and feel depressed that I buckled and drank again. Before I know it I'll be back on that treadmill of wine buying, wine drinking, wine recovery. I'll be back living that awful wine-fuelled nightmarish life.'

The pitch of my voice is increasing as I talk and I'm speeding up. I'm bursting with crazy energy, I'm fizzing and fired up and I need to do something! Anything but drink! What's a girl to do to get through this? How can I shut up the noise in my head and not bloody drink?

Clean. I clean. I put my yellow rubber gloves on and for the next two hours I clean our goddamn house from top to bottom. The bathroom gets scrubbed, the floors get vacuumed, the surfaces get polished, the toys get cleared away. I am a crazy determined non-drinking cleaning freak. There is no stopping me.

Mrs D Is Going Without (Day 41)

I cleaned until I sat on the sofa at 7.30 p.m. puffed out (yes, I was puffed from all this hard-out cleaning!) with a ginger beer and read recovery blogs from other people and ordered recovery books from the library catalogue online.

It was hard, but I won.

I won!!!!!!!

It's the next morning when I write up the story of my Saturday night battle with the pang-to-beat-all-pangs and click 'publish' to send it out into the world. I fought the cravings, beat them down with my yellow rubber gloves, survived yet another sober day and got to write all about it in a blog post. All of this feels very nice in a low-key satisfying way. But oh wow, what comes back to me from out in the world, through the internet and onto my computer screen over the next few days makes it all the more satisfying. Like the most magical fairy dust that has ever been invented, a wave of love and support arrives as comments on my blog:

Comment from 'Nan'
That is awesome . . . great job. Stay strong!

Comment from 'Nate'
Well done for putting that voice to bed.

Comment from 'WritingTheBoozeAway'
Yea for you!!! What you did is called addictive voice recognition technique. I recall my mind whirled around stopping by the store every damn night to buy vodka for months, until, suddenly, it stopped! Non-judgemental, mindful awareness worked for me. Cheers! It's all so worth it!

Comment from 'Trying to Be Normal'
I echo what WritingTheBoozeAway wrote—one day the thoughts become less powerful, naggy and loud. Keep on keeping on—it does get easier.

Sweet mana from the internet. I don't know if these people leaving comments have any idea what a huge difference they are making to my life. I feel totally jazzed that they're following along with me, helping me, teaching me.

'Addictive voice recognition technique' someone said. What is that? I google it to find out more. Okay, so apparently addictive voice recognition technique (AVRT) is a dissociative technique (that's psychology talk) whereby you identify the addictive voice inside your mind and then you separate from it. The internet tells me I need to think of my internal addict like a naughty child or a nasty acquaintance, a separate being that lives inside of me. All it wants is for me to drink more, and when I don't drink it's goading me on. It wants me all to itself. And ratting on it is a great way to cut some of its power. That's what I did!

Mrs D Is Going Without (Day 46)
I like this. I feel like I've been telling on my addict in this blog which is why I started writing this blog. I've written about how my addict drove me to pick up wine bottles even when I was trying to have an alcohol-free day, how

my addict would do deals with itself over hangovers ('I can drink lots tonight and have a hangover tomorrow because I'm not going to the gym, then that hangover will stop me drinking too much tomorrow night which is good because I want to go to the gym the next day after that'), how my addict would appear behind my eyes like a paranoid junkie whenever the wine started to be drunk, checking out how much was left ('How much are they having? How much is left for me? How much is in the house? How much can I get? *I'm your addict and I need lots of wine!!!*') I'm telling tales on my stupid fucking addict to get her out of my head for good (hopefully).

I'm feeling so great that I've got this fun, secret, helpful blog vibe happening. It's out-of-this-world unbelievably cool. I decide I can't keep it a secret from Corin anymore. I can't live keeping secrets from Corin (well, clearly I can't because hiding a bottle of wine from him sent me into a complete tail-spin and sparked a monumental life change). I need to tell him about my blog now; to keep it a secret from him any longer would just be weird and wrong.

I do it at lunchtime on Monday when he's just home from the TVNZ studios. He's exhausted, as he always is after presenting on-air for three straight hours, standing in the kitchen making a huge feast to eat before falling into bed for an afternoon nap.

'Honey,' I slowly begin, 'I've got something to tell you.'

'Yes,' he replies warily, probably mentally preparing himself to hear some sort of dramatic statement from me.

'Um, well,' I continue, 'I actually have this thing going on which I've kept a secret till now because I was just really nervous and focused and determined and . . .' I'm babbling. Corin has stopped making his sandwich and is staring at me.

'What?' he says.

'Um, oh, it's not bad or anything, it's just that I started a blog when I stopped drinking.' I feel a bit stupid now, like it's not that big a deal. 'I've been writing in it most days, like in the morning mostly, just writing what's happening for me with the not-drinking and what I'm feeling and stuff. Just writing, you know, to try and, um, help me to not drink ever again.'

'Oh! Good idea,' Corin says, taking a big mouthful of his sandwich, probably relieved that I didn't tell him I was going to start drinking again or run off to India to do a five-week retreat or something.

'Yeah, but the thing is, now something really cool is happening and some people are actually reading it and . . . I've been getting some comments from people. Like, people are helping me now.'

'Wow,' says Corin, and he's obviously impressed at this. 'Who are they?'

'I dunno,' I reply, picking at his food even though I've already eaten. 'Some of them are anonymous, some have their own blogs, some just put a name but you can't figure out who they are. But they're all being really nice to me, which is cool.'

'That's so great!' he says. I can tell he's pleased I'm happy and upbeat for the first time in a long time. And I figure he's probably relieved to hear I've got somewhere to vent other than just talking to him. Poor guy does spend an awful lot of time listening to me blah on about booze and all the endlessly fascinating stuff that I am reading and thinking and discovering (well, at least I think it's endlessly fascinating). I'm sure he's pleased I've got another outlet for all my brain noise.

He wipes his hands and sits at the computer to take a look around my blog, reading some of the latest posts and seeing how there are a few comments here and there. I hover around behind him, feeling a bit vulnerable, but I think he's quietly proud of what I've gone and set up, and if he finds it weird that I've kept it a secret until now he doesn't let on. 'Isn't it great that there are people in similar situations to you around this blogging space?' he says and gives me a big hug before heading off for a nap.

I tidy up the kitchen and think about how lucky I am to have someone like Corin alongside me right now. He's consistently very calm and stable, which is a godsend at the best of times but particularly lately with me being all over the show emotionally. He just listens and listens and listens and never complains or criticises or judges me for anything. He's totally engaged in what I'm doing, but in a lovingly detached way, not interfering or dictating how he thinks I should be dealing with stuff. And he's never once complained about the fact that he's now married to a non-drinker—he married a boozy party girl, remember?! Luckily (unless he's hiding it really well) he doesn't seem to mind that I'm completely changing my ways.

However I am, it must be said, working really hard to make him feel he doesn't need to change along with me by buying him wine every now and then. My attitude is that this is my problem and my problem alone. I'm the one that can't control or moderate my booze. Alcohol is going to be all around me for the rest of my life, I might as well get used to having it in the house, too. I just have to focus on fixing me.

Speaking of me (as if I haven't enough already), I'm actually now starting to lift up again and feel really good about this new non-drinking lifestyle. Great, in fact. So great it's almost like I'm on some sort of high. I'm positively soaring along. I'd even go so far as to say, I feel elated!

Is it because I'm getting the odd comment here and there on my blog? Is it because my body has adjusted to being a wine-free temple? Is it because my nasty pimple has cleared and the great night's sleep I'm regularly getting is starting to have an impact? Or is it because since my Oprah revelation I've slowly been realising the full impact my steady, heavy wine-drinking was having on my life?

I think it's all of the above, but mostly I think it's because of what started dawning on me after the Oprah moment. I'm starting to look at my drinking differently. I'm starting to make sense of the emotional lurching all-over-the-show that I've been doing over the past few weeks. Me being overly emotional without the wine is showing me how unemotional I was with it.

Getting angry with Corin the other night wasn't fun and I felt decidedly uncomfortable about it. But now I'm looking back at that evening and thinking, 'That was anger, I felt angry.' Some rough days with the kids have had me stressed and, boy, do I want to drink on those days. But now I'm looking back and thinking, 'That was stress, I felt stressed.' Some days I feel inexplicably flat. Just flat and glum. But now I'm looking at those days and thinking, 'Sadness, is this what sadness feels like?' I'm just starting to realise that I never really allowed myself the space to feel anything much. Not anger or stress or sadness. I just glug, glug, glugged wine all the time without considering its full impact. Wine levelled me, it smoothed me out.

Now I've been sober for a while I can see how my life is going to be different. I'm going to feel more, be far more attuned to my moods. Life without wine is more up and down, and I was avoiding that. My steady, heavy wine-drinking was not just a habit gone too far but a life choice. And now I'm choosing something different. It all seems so much easier to read. This dawning realisation is so amazing I feel uplifted. I feel clearer. Hang on . . . clarity. This is clarity! Holy shit, this is the clarity people talk about!

I'm so giddy at my realisation that I start talking more widely with friends about how I'm feeling. Walking the kids home from school one day, I joke with a fellow mum about my newfound clarity. 'When I used to hear people talk about gaining clarity, I thought it meant that because they weren't hungover all the time they could open their eyes more widely to see better.' I'm laughing wildly as I explain to her, 'I thought "seeing more clearly" meant you could literally see better without your eyes being blurry ha ha ha!' I am highly amused at my own stupidity. I'm not sure that my friend is matching my amusement levels but she's listening and being very kind. 'Now I'm starting to realise that having clarity means you can actually understand yourself and your moods better. Does that make sense?' I ask her as we cross the road with a gaggle of small children around us but don't give her a chance to reply. 'I just feel like I'm starting to get what my drinking was all about, like it wasn't just that I wanted everything to be fun all the time, it was also that I didn't want to feel anything slightly negative.' Oh the joy

I feel at relaying this amazing revelation. God knows what my friend must have been thinking.

Mrs D Is Going Without (Day 51)

Every morning I wake up feeling clear, and I am starting to relax and accept that this new clear-headedness is with me to stay, I am embracing the new sober me and I like her.

I re-read my old diary this week and it was so sad to read teenage me writing about hating myself, and getting drunk all the time, and hating myself. Miserable teenage me. I want to go back in time and give teenage Mrs D a big hug and whisper in her ear, 'It's okay, I'm going to get you through' . . . because I did get me through and look at me now!

Sorry for this arrogance talking but I'm feeling empowered by my decision to remove alcohol from my life and really happy and proud of myself that I am doing it. I feel like this is my only life, this is it, and I'm living it how I want to. That's a great feeling and long may it last.

Of course, it doesn't.

12

Apparently, there's a name for this elation I'm feeling. My wise wonderful blog readers inform me that this giddy high I am on is actually a known phenomenon in early sobriety and it's got the delightfully cheerful name of 'pink cloud'. I'm floating on a pink cloud, baby!

Comment from 'Derek'

The pink cloud is that wonderful time in early recovery when it all starts clicking and the using days seem far behind and life is just great, great, great ... it's a good thing, but also kinda dangerous, cos we start to consider ourselves ten foot tall and bulletproof ... and start to think we got this clean and sober thing nailed ... and get a little too big for our britches.

Right, so I have to prepare myself for this feeling to end,

but that can happen later . . . for now I just want to enjoy it. Pink clouds rock!

I feel happy and light for the first time in ages. Clever me! I feel empowered by my growing understanding of what my drinking was all about. It sounds cheesy and clichéd to say, but coming to this realisation is totally awesome and utterly unexpected. I'm sure that's why it's so powerful, because I've come to it myself. I bet that if someone had tried to sit me down six months ago and tell me that my steady wine consumption was me choosing to not properly deal with any emotional shit, I would have laughed at them or gotten really pissed off. Certainly I wouldn't have heard it properly or believed it. But because the realisation has come to me via me, because it's me figuring me out, me educating myself, it's unbelievably powerful—hence the giddy feeling. *Woohoo!!!*

I'm kind of wide-eyed in amazement. Now I know that taking the booze away isn't just about me breaking a habit, it's actually about me having to approach life differently. Without alcohol entering my system all the time, I always have to deal with shit in a raw state, and never reach for my beloved liquid cope-all. It feels amazing to understand this.

But I can also sense why I'm being warned that this pink cloud feeling isn't going to last—I have to move forward and actually do this. Dealing with shit, raw, all the time, forever. Actually live through every single day feeling every single feeling that comes at me and never drinking to escape. And not just bad shit like anger and stress and sadness. Good shit, too, like elation and triumph and joy. All of it, all the time, raw. No big glasses of red wine to take the edge off a stressful day, no flutes of bubbles to toast in celebration, no cold beer to welcome in summer, no whiskey to loosen tongues on a late-night confessional. Looking ahead into my life and imagining dealing with everything in a raw state is somewhat overwhelming. I can't bear to look too far ahead so I just lie back and luxuriate on my beautiful pink cloud.

The timing of this pink cloud couldn't be better, actually— we're still in the middle of our full-on phase of socialising, starting tonight with a huge black-tie gala dinner that's being held in honour of Sir Richard Branson. Yes, the Virgin dude is in town. Corin and I usually turn down invites to glitzy functions (we can't be bothered), but this one we have to go to because Corin's been asked to interview Sir Richard on stage in front of all the dinner guests. It's a big honour.

I'm not too nervous as I get ready. In a funny way, knowing ahead of time that I won't be drinking at the dinner makes me feel more secure in how I'm going to be. I can rest assured that I won't be chasing the wines all evening like I normally do. I'm careful to make sure my dress (borrowed) isn't on inside out but sadly I neglect to practise walking in my new high heels. So it's not until we're approaching the venue that I realise they're too big. My heels keep lifting out of the back of them, which is causing me to shuffle awkwardly—this is not classy.

I manage to walk in okay by clinging onto Corin's arm, trying very hard not to care about how silly I must look shuffling along. The venue is decorated beautifully and packed to the gunnels with all manner of gorgeous and glamorous people (Rachel Hunter!), the rich and famous, and breakfast TV hosts with their newly sober wives. We find our table at the front and sit down. The room is buzzing and I nervously ask a passing waiter for a non-alcoholic drink. When she returns with it I ask her to snap a photo of Corin and me on my phone, and I send it to Corin's mum with the accompanying text: 'Out at a posh dinner!'

I start to relax and, well, I actually start to enjoy myself. There are some nice businessmen at the table with us and they are chatty and low-key. No one is really boozing and it seems irrelevant that my drink is a soft one. The entree comes around and after I've gobbled it down (it's all about the food when I'm not drinking) I shuffle off to the bathroom as fast as I can so I don't miss Corin's star turn, which is coming up next. In the ladies' toilet I encounter a couple of very made-up, glamorous women acting quite aggressively tipsy. I'm quietly pleased to notice that inwardly I'm not envying their booziness at all (although I bet their shoes fit).

I'm so incredibly proud of Corin when he takes to the stage to interview Sir Richard and he does a great job. He comes back to the table happy, we eat the main course and then decide to abandon the glitterati, slip out early and head home. Corin does have an early-morning wake-up ahead of him we tell ourselves, but really we've just had enough. And I need to get these shoes off pronto.

Mrs D Is Going Without (Day 53)

Went to a big glitzy function last night, oh so very posh, and had a couple of delicious lemon drinks and an orange juice. No problems! Usually at a function like that I'd be chasing the wines and my regrets the next morning would be 'Who saw that I was boozing?' But today, no worries!

It's interesting looking back on this night because I don't feel like I was missing out on anything by not-drinking. But then again it wasn't exactly a warm fun crowd full of friends and family, either. And maybe the pink cloud was buoying me along.

Over the next few days, however, I fear my cloud's buoyancy is starting to fade and the cold hard reality of trying to never drink again is once more hitting home. It's the bloody Rugby World Cup that's got me glum again. The All Blacks have made it through to the finals (thankfully, I'm not sure New Zealand would have coped if they hadn't) and the Biggest Party Ever In The History Of Our Nation is once again being planned for game night. It cannot be ignored so we've invited a bunch of friends over to watch it at our house.

While Corin and the boys get busy moving furniture around to create a stadium in our living room, I go to the supermarket for supplies. The place is heaving and there's a real buzz in the air; everyone's really excited and nervous about the big game. I grab chips and dip and yeast for the pizza bases and deliberately skirt widely around the booze aisle (Corin has already stocked up in this department). It's a good thing I don't need to go down there because it's like Grand Central Station. It's packed! Booze, booze, so much booze is being piled into so many trolleys. And this is just in my neighbourhood at this particular time of the day. Around the country all day long this will be going on. I think about all the collective litres of alcohol that are going to be poured down the throats of my countrymen and women tonight and it's a lot.

But not my delicate sober throat, I think to myself as I grab a couple of energy drinks by the checkout. I won't lie, I do feel a bit sad about that. I do feel a bit flat. It's not exactly happy-happy-joy-joy in my head right now. Just a sort of sad determination. I'm adjusting still, I tell myself. I have no choice, I tell myself. This is just the way it has to be, I tell myself.

The evening passes fine, I don't drink, and thank goodness the All Blacks win.

Mrs D Is Going Without (Day 56)

So life is different without alcohol in it. Not surprising given the amount of hours I devoted to wine (planning, acquiring, drinking, recovering) that are now wine-less hours. But aside from the expected and happy results of living sober—less guilt, fewer headaches and sick guts, more money in the bank—there are other results that I hadn't expected.

So what are they? I've been spending the last few days trying to put my finger on what is different and how it is that I feel different. Well, there's one answer right there. I'm definitely more introspective, looking inside my mind more to analyse how I'm feeling. I've never been a huge navel-gazer, but I am more so now. As I said to my sister-in-law the other night, you feel more when you're not drinking.

Clearer? I've heard other people say they feel so much clearer without alcohol and I think I understand what that means. But I'd also describe it as flat at times. Or empty. Just a wide open life without any mind bending. All that time I've spent with my brain altered by alcohol, now it's just a big wide open brain that isn't inebriated. Sometimes that's a good thing. Other times, not so good. Last few days I've been tired and grouchy and feeling a bit low. A week or so ago I was feeling awesome and talking about pink clouds. So more highs and lows. Yeah. More highs and lows.

Problem is I'm not so good at sitting with a 'wide-open' brain. I seem to need to keep myself constantly mentally stimulated. Wine stimulated me . . . or numbed me . . . or both . . . which obviously appealed to me. But now that I'm not spending many hours under wine's influence I've got a lot of free brain time. I need to find more things to keep my mind occupied.

Comment from 'Nate'

One of the challenges is to re-allocate that time into something productive and fulfilling. I have flat and empty periods and almost mourn the alcohol-less future.

Try buying some new walking shoes and start walking around the neighbourhood. Works for me. Every time in the afternoon I feel I could/should/used to be drinking, I walk to the beach and that certainly clears my head.

It's a great idea, but sadly looking after small boys every day means I don't have the sort of lifestyle that allows for walks to the beach when I feel like it. Don't get me wrong, I love looking after our gorgeous sons, but it does mean I don't have a lot of completely free hours to myself (only free thinking hours punctuated by regular interactions with the kids). It's the housewife's eternal quandary, crazy busy all the time but also strangely bored. Boozing worked well to solve that quandary by taking me away mentally while not taking me away physically.

But that faux-escape is not available to me any more. So I need to find more to do with my brain now I'm sober, while also continuing to be a domestic goddess and the perfect wife and mother (ha ha).

Reading other sober blogs is helping to fill my time. I've discovered quite a few of them. I'm learning that there is a small but very active online community of sober bloggers and blog readers, and I've been warmly welcomed into that. I figure out how to put a 'Blog List' down the left-hand side of my own site that links to other blogs and automatically updates when people have written new posts. It makes my own blog all the more active and alive. Fun! And I add a couple of new pages to my site with some information about me and the books that I'm reading. My online life is humming along nicely and there's no doubt it is doing wonders to get me through the days. Writing, reading, commenting, it's all helping to keep me away from the wine.

Overall, right now, I feel like I'm doing okay, but not great. 'Okay' because I haven't had a drink since I decided to stop, but 'not great' because I'm still lurching all over the show. Isn't life's goal to be smooth and calm all the time and not up and down? It feels to me like all of this bloody emoting is somehow a failure. It's uncomfortable for me, I want to be smooth and calm all the time and not grumpy or sad or stressed or whatever. I have no idea what is normal anymore. What I thought was a normal way of living was clearly not, given I maintained it with the help of crap-loads of wine. So what's normal now? I'm confused. This sober-living thing is endlessly fascinating, I'll be honest, but it's not comfortable by any stretch of the imagination.

13

There is one big positive, though; one major thing that I am definitely not struggling with anymore—and that is the lonely feeling I used to overwhelmingly have. I'm anything but lonely in my sober endeavours now thanks to my blog and the wonderful faceless online community growing up around it. Comments regularly trickle in from blog readers, and every one contains a tiny nugget of gold and gives me a little stab of joy. Some make me cry, some make me think, some teach me, some challenge me. But they all connect with me and every single one feels like a lovely cyber hug. How could I possibly feel lonely when I'm getting cyber hugged all day every day!

Comment from 'Bento'

Hi! I'm also trying to stop drinking. I can relate to much of what you have posted. Hang in there.

Comment from 'Macy'

I see myself over and over in your blog ... it helps to know I'm not alone in my quitting-drinking journey ... thank you.

Comment from 'Natasha'

I love your post and the way I can relate to you ... you and I are 'the same kind of drinker' ... only after 5 p.m. most nights. Not a binger, just steady ...

Lots of comments are like these ones from Bento, Macy and Natasha. Little 'I'm in the same boat' messages.

Comment from 'Anonymous'

I love reading your blog. I needed to find something that I could connect to that would help me overcome this addiction ... I knew from the first night that I bought a bottle of wine and brought it home to drink while making dinner. I still remember that moment ... about 12 years ago ... when I started drinking at home. I knew that was a turning point ... a bad one ... in my life. It escalated fast. And now this is another turning point ... a good one. Thank you for helping me by sharing your journey.

And so often I get these thankyous from people. 'Thank you for sharing', they say. I'm not going to lie, it feels incredible that writing my own experiences is helping others. I did not expect this.

Comment from 'Anonymous'

Hi Mrs D. I love your blog! I stayed up way too late last night reading the whole thing. We seem to have a lot in common. I, too, am a 40-year-old mum of boys, on my second round of sobriety after erroneously pronouncing myself cured after almost one year off the sauce. Er ... no ... not cured, and it's harder to stop the second time around.

Putting aside the kindness and warmth from this anonymous reader, this comment is bloody scary and works well to keep me on my toes. She gave up for a whole year and then returned to drinking thinking she was cured ... but she wasn't, and stopping for the second time was harder. *Harder?!* How could it possibly be harder than what I'm going through now? I'm not bloody doing this all over again. I will never consider myself cured. A great message gratefully received.

Comment from 'Milly'

I, too, have ended a 20+ year (actually more like 30) affair with booze but my favourite poison was bourbon.

It's always interesting to hear what other people's particular 'poison' is. My favourite tipple was red wine—any variety so long as it was red. For Judy it was white wine . . .

Comment from 'Judy'

I relate to almost every single word you write. I am a 40-something mother-of-one with a lovely husband (who can drink just one beer or less and be happy). White wine is my poison. I want to be one of those people who can take it or leave it. There is no question that my habit impacts my life, my body, my relationships, my work performance—ugh, the dreaded weekday hangover. Why isn't that enough of a deterrent?

Keep sharing. You are a talented writer and I, for one, am inspired by the candid account of your thoughts on this journey. It's time for a change.

Yes Judy, it is time for a change! I inwardly cry when I read her comment, basking in the glow of her compliment about my writing. This is a nice comment to get not just for the praise but because there are so many similarities in our stories. Judy was never deterred by hangovers (I'm always gobsmacked when people tell me imagining the next-day hangover is enough to stop them drinking), she is also married to a 'normal' drinker and would love to be that way. I think about Judy long after she's posted her comment and ponder her desire to be someone who can 'take or leave' alcohol—a moderate drinker, not someone fixated with wine. I'm not sure that we can ever be those people. I think my moderation button was broken at birth.

Comment from 'Toni'

I'm not sure what the statistics are for housewives or women in general but I'll admit to secretly drinking when I stayed home with my young daughter. I joined the workforce in May and my drinking escalated.

I love hearing from other parents who are getting sober. It makes me very happy for all of our kids. And it's not just mothers who are reaching out to me.

Comment from 'Nate'

'I don't miss yelling at the boys to stop yelling because my head is pounding.' This much is true. Sad that I was always yelling at them bloody kids cos they wanted to play with me when I was busy getting drunk.

Glad that shit is all behind me.

Comment from 'FacingUpToTheFacts'

Hi Mrs D. It sounds like I'm a male version of yourself, just starting this journey. I'll be reading your blog from start to finish with interest!

Sometimes readers offer me different ways of looking at sobriety . . .

Comment from 'Anonymous'

Mrs D I enjoy reading your blog and your honesty. Keep up the good work. I look at drinking now as a break-up—aka a relationship gone bad. It's not always easy to break up but in the long run we know it's the best thing to do for our sanity! ;-)

Sometimes they offer me alternative drink options . . .

Comment from 'Miriam'

In my first year sober, I made homemade ginger beer, not very sweet, and also a drink with soda and fresh lime juice with a crushed stalk of lemongrass in it to infuse flavour. It was fun and assuaged the need I felt then for comforting drinks because I couldn't imagine going anywhere without a drink in my hand.

Sometimes they reveal they haven't yet summoned the courage to quit . . .

Comment from 'Janet'

Hi! I love your blog so far! I can completely relate . . . except I'm still drinking and trying to stop. I even made a 'promise' to have a drink-free November, but that lasted about 2 hours. So I've started re-reading all the addiction blogs and am going to try this on my own. Thanks so much for sharing!

And sometimes they reveal themselves as a fellow sober blogger.

Comment from 'AMothersJourney'
Just came across your blog. Congrats on making the big step! Looking forward to reading up some more about how you have been doing. I hope you find blogging helpful. It's helped me a lot in the past 2 years of my sobriety.

I have to keep updating my Blog List to feature new sober bloggers as I discover them, so that visitors to my site can see all the sober bloggers' new posts as they are written. It's great being able to offer readers of my blog access not just to my experiences, but the experiences of other former boozers as well. It's astounding to me how many people seem to be floating around the internet looking for help with drinking, and because visitors to my blog are so kind and nice I love offering them as much as I can.

Comment from 'TheGirlIUsedToBe'
I think you are so, so brave. You can do this, you owe it to yourself to be happy. And you will be :-)

Comment from 'Anonymous'

Mrs D keep posting. I look forward to reading your blog daily. Your words are helping more people than you know . . . including me!

Comment from 'Sunny'

Dear Mrs D, Love your blog. You could be me. Putting down the drink is almost the easy bit. Living sober is the hard bit.

Yes Sunny, as I am about to discover, living sober can be extremely hard.

14

Suddenly my pink cloud dissipates completely and dumps me in a steaming pile of emotional shit that I am ill-equipped to deal with.

First I learn that I have hurt a friend's feelings by doing something thoughtless involving a kid's party. When I hear (through a mutual friend) that she is offended, I'm utterly mortified so I rush over to her house and blurt out a teary apology on her doorstep: '(sob sob) I'm so sorry I didn't mean to hurt you (sob sob) you're so lovely I don't want you to be upset (sob sob) I can't believe I didn't properly think it through (sob sob) how you would react (sniff sniff) sorry I'm crying I'm just really emotional right now (sniff sniff) it's the not-drinking (sniff sniff) but I'm just so sorry I hurt you (sniff).'

Honestly, who the fuck is this thoughtless, emotional, dramatic woman masquerading as me?

My friend does seem a little taken aback by my outpouring of emotion but also thankful for the apology. As I drive home I feel okay about it, actually . . . if nothing else, she can't accuse me of being unfeeling!

Then Corin heads out one evening to attend another big glitzy event but this time without me—it's the New Zealand Music Awards. He is reluctant to go but ends up having a great night because his brother and some mates are there and they all get a bit tipsy and rock'n'roll on it. Back at home I, on the other hand, find myself getting slowly more and more wound up to the point where I am a seething mass of grumpiness. Normally when Corin goes out without me I throw myself a little party all on my own. (Logic = so I don't miss out! See me having fun in my living room drinking bubbles all alone! Glug, glug, glug.) Well, not anymore.

So, with Corin out and me deprived of the opportunity to party alone, I slowly get more tense and angry as the evening progresses. About exactly what I'm not sure. There is a good reason floating around my brain somewhere. It probably doesn't help that I'm watching the broadcast of the awards on TV and following along on Twitter so I'm really aware of the *fun party* that is going on without me and how *goddamn sober* I am. I can't bear the thought that this is my reality forevermore.

By the time poor Corin rolls in around 1 a.m. I've worked myself into a complete state. He comes into the bedroom, tired and wobbly, telling me about his night. 'At the start there was a VIP entrance with fans and media and stuff and because I'm on tele I got pushed towards it even though I just wanted to slip in quietly. It was so weird, like an actual red carpet.' He's giggling now as he tells me the story. 'I really didn't feel comfortable acting like a star, talking to fans and being interviewed and stuff so I ran down it instead! I just up and ran!' This is actually quite funny but in my state of grumpy woe-is-me-itis I am in no mood to laugh and instead I explode.

I throw a complete hissy-fit about everything that is wrong with this picture and the part he's playing in it. I'm emoting like a crazy harridan who has been in a coma for twenty years. All of this anger comes out my mouth and tears are pouring from my eyes and I rip back the bedcovers and storm across the room in a rage. Poor Corin, I don't think he quite knows what's going on. I pause briefly to tear my dressing gown off the back of the door but do it so violently that the metal hook holding the gown snaps in half. This kind of ruins the moment because I have to stop and pick up the broken bit. I'm gutted the hook is broken but I don't want to ruin my dramatic exit so I continue to storm out of the bedroom and into the living room where—fuming—I lie on the couch as if I'm going to sleep there.

Who the fuck am I?

So now I'm kind of huddled on the sofa in my dressing

gown with a broken hook in my hand and it's cold and dark in the living room (I didn't think to get a blanket) and I'm a bit stuck on what to do next. And I'm a bit confused as to what's actually going on. I'm mad as all hell, but what at? Is it something Corin's done? Or is it at myself for making this stupid goddamn decision not to drink and now having to live with the difficult consequences of that decision? Consequences like sitting at home alone with no wine to fill the space. Why can't I cope with empty space?

Luckily for me a tired and bemused Corin appears in the living room after a short while and says simply, 'Sweetie, come to bed,' and because I'm cold I do and eventually we fall asleep.

Mrs D Is Going Without (Day 60)

I am a different woman. I seriously am. I cry all the time. My self-image has been rocked to its core. I feel shaky. Before giving up the sauce I thought I was fine, but lately I've been feeling like a boring loser, stuck at home with a wobbly tummy and no value.

Is all this drama the new normal? Is this how I'm always going to live from now on? I didn't sign up to this.

Comment from 'Anonymous'

Dear Mrs D, don't worry, this is normal (for an alcoholic

:-)) It will pass as long as you don't drink. Think of it as a healing crisis.

This is the stuff the alcohol was suppressing. Alcoholism is not just a physical addiction, it is a mental, emotional and spiritual illness. The drink is just a symptom. Stay strong!

Comment from 'Anonymous'

The commenter above is right! This IS normal and you will eventually feel better. You've been drowning your emotions for a while and you need time for them to even out.

The last thing you need is to stifle them again. I like the comment 'Think of it as a healing crisis'. How true!!

Comment from 'Anonymous'

Oh, Mrs D you sound like you're right on track! Sorry, don't mean to make light of your difficult time. Hey, go easy on yourself. You are experiencing a massive shift in how you live your life—there's bound to be some bumps and drama involved.

Comment from 'Miriam'

Sympathy to you—while I was drinking I had no idea why I drank, had many theories but no definite idea. Then I sobered up and began finding out how I really felt and how much I had relied on drinking as a buffer and pick-me-up and crude anaesthetic. I drank to find out how I was feeling, I drank to escape feeling, I drank to shift the feelings. Sober I discovered that years of alcohol abuse had flattened all my emotions like a thick layer of concrete—they came back like a rollercoaster before settling down.

Bless my beautiful commenters. I can so relate to what Miriam is saying. It is like a thick layer of concrete has been lifted off me and it does feel like I'm on some sort of god-awful rollercoaster. I fucking hate rollercoasters; they scare the shit out of me. I'm the person who stands at the bottom holding the coats. Now I'm strapped in, hurtling along at breakneck speed. I'm really uncomfortable with all this goddamn emotion. 'A healing crisis', one of my helpful commenters said. I like that, too. It helps me to see this as a phase. Maybe it won't last forever. I'm going through a healing crisis and I just need to take it easy right now, look after myself and move gently through the days.

Only one problem: my stepbrother's Indian-themed wedding is tonight. Shitballs! My eyes are red-rimmed from all the crying I've been doing and I'm exhausted with the lack of sleep that resulted from my stupid tantrum. I feel fat and ugly and messy and wound up and not in the mood to wear a bloody sari! Instead I rush out to the mall and buy a tonne of sparkly plastic bracelets and a bindi to stick on my forehead. Then I pop over to a mate's house and borrow a skirt that should work for an Indian-themed wedding. Alright, the skirt isn't Indian at all; it looks more like a Thai Airways uniform. The fabric is an ornate purple and gold and it's cut in a tight tube straight down to the floor. It's so tight I can barely take proper steps in it but rather only small shuffling ones—what is it with me and bloody shuffling along at parties?

At least I can drive to the wedding knowing that I'm going to be sober all night. This is surprisingly incredibly satisfying. No taxi fare wasted! I'll take this good feeling. I need all the good feelings I can get right now, because overall I'm still feeling quite grumpy. We pick up my sister and brother-in-law on the way to the venue and I'm trying to appear cheerful, turning up the music in the car as we cross the harbour bridge. But pulling into the venue carpark and seeing other wedding guests arriving in their lovely sparkly saris displaying toned midriffs and tanned shoulders is not helping. I feel uncomfortable in my unsexy airhostess uniform but force a smile onto my face for the sake of the groom and his lovely wife-to-be. Just get through, I tell myself. Just get through and don't drink.

Lots of my family are here, my dad and two of my sisters and their husbands. Are they all aware this is my first sober wedding? Probably not. It's highly likely I'm the only person in the room obsessed with the fact that I'm not drinking tonight.

Wrong. After the ceremony Dad quietly lets me know that he's not going to drink tonight—'in solidarity with you, darling'—which is bloody nice of him and really does work to make me feel better. Normally I'd be hooking into the free booze by now (like most people seem to be) but instead I nervously fetch a lemonade from the bar and try to settle myself down. Corin has been latched onto by some fans of *Breakfast* so he's having to chat away and be polite but I'm not in a mingling mood at all. And neither, it emerges, are my sisters and my dad—hooray! Instead we clump ourselves together in a corner and quietly chat away. I'm aware we're being a bit antisocial but I don't mind, it's so nice to be surrounded by family, making jokes, rating the canapés and checking out all the beautiful saris. We do manage to tear ourselves away from our corner to approach the bride and offer our congratulations. She looks so happy and radiant I start to realise that this isn't a day about me and not-drinking, it's a day about them. That makes me feel a bit better.

I do still feel really odd that I'm not drinking. It sounds like nothing much, but for a hardcore boozer like me this is *huge*! I could so easily walk over to the bar and order a wine or a bubbles. No one is stopping me. I'm on a self-imposed sobriety mission. Am I crazy?

I stand chewing a mini pakora with raita (tasty, definitely a nine out of ten) and think back to all the past weddings I have attended. So many of them I have written myself off at. I run through them in my mind, trying to remember what I was like at each one: drunk, drunk, drunk, pregnant, drunk, drunk (vomited), drunk, pregnant, drunk, drunk, drunk (lost a shoe), drunk, drunk. Holy shit! I think every wedding I've attended I got drunk at unless I was up the duff. Even my own bloody wedding was an all-nighter. So this one tonight, with no baby in my belly and no booze either, it's a huge deal.

The MC calls for everyone to make their way to their tables. 'The speeches will start in fifteen minutes,' he says. I shuffle up the winding staircase (I have to cling hard to the banister because my skirt is so tight) and around the mezzanine level to find where we are sitting. Then I start acting like a freak.

15

My brother-in-law and Corin have come upstairs without drinks. This is a travesty (says my twisted boozer's mind). 'I'll get you one!' I chirp.

'Nah, don't worry,' they say. 'The bar's miles away.'

'No, seriously, it's fine!' I chirp again and proceed to stand up and shuffle in my ridiculous skirt back around the mezzanine level, inch slowly down the winding staircase holding tight to the banister, and shuffle across the foyer to the bar, where I chirpily order two beers. I collect the drinks and shuffle back across the foyer to the stairs and awkwardly inch my way up them, not able to hold the banister because my hands are full of *alcohol for other people!* What the hell am I doing? Desperately trying to prove I'm still cool with other people drinking? Desperate for other people to get drunk because that's what I imagine everyone wants to do at a wedding? Desperate to keep busy? Just generally desperate?

I make it to the top of the stairs and shuffle back around the mezzanine level to our table and deliver the drinks. I think everyone is a bit bemused but I am hair-flicking-ly okay. 'No problem,' I chirp (even my chirping is odd). Then I notice a couple of other people sitting at the table have finished their drinks so *I do it again!!!* Around, down, across, shuffle, inch, shuffle, across, up, around, shuffle, inch, shuffle, chirp, chirp, chirp.

Freak.

Luckily the wedding juggernaut takes over and there's speeches to listen to and food to eat (curry—yum!), and just as the party is really about to kick off my darling nephew comes to my rescue. He's at my sister's house refusing to settle with his babysitter so I offer to drive my sister back to him (and continue on home myself). It's just 9.30 p.m. as we quietly say our goodbyes (Corin elects to stay) and slip out. I hope no one minds.

It's pouring with rain as we exit the venue so we sprint to the car laughing wildly. I've got my tight skirt hitched up and I'm feeling good. I did it! I may have acted like a weird alcohol-delivering freak and bailed early, but I did it. I did my first wedding sober! I feel great!

I can't help myself (never can) and start babbling away to my sister about how amazing it feels to have stayed sober and to be driving myself home. 'It's such a revelation to see how I don't just have to drink all the time,' I burble over the flapping windscreen wipers. 'I thought I did but I don't. This is a whole new world to me. I'm so happy I'm figuring this out. All I used to do was drink, drink, drink. Unquestionably drink all the time. Now I've stopped and it's so fascinating what I'm learning. I keep questioning why I drank so much all the time and the answers that are coming are so unexpected. It's amazing. I mean, I've been really fucking emotional lately so it's not always amazing, sometimes it's really shitty and hard, but right now I feel amazing!' I'm raving and a bit giddy but I can't stop myself. I'm ecstatic that I'm driving myself home from this wedding and I'm sober. Another small victory!

My sister just sits there quietly, listening to me and watching all this emotion flow out of me, and then she says gently: 'I don't know why I'm thinking this right now but I feel like if you'd kept drinking, one day you would have just burst into tears without knowing why and never been able to stop.'

She doesn't know how right she is. If I had kept boozing and my feelings had stayed squashed, maybe one day they would have burst out of me uncontrollably. I'll never know because now I'm cracking away at the concrete myself. And, boy, are my emotions flooding out. Right now, driving home from a wedding in the rain, I'm so happy. Last night I was breaking hooks and slamming doors. This is the new normal. I'm waking up.

But then I come crashing down, my inner addict throws a hissy-fit and I get hit with an intense longing.

Mrs D Is Going Without (Day 65)

The longing to drink first came in a moment of stillness, which is very interesting, actually. My busy weekend was very lovely and calming and I found myself on Sunday evening in a pleasant relaxed state after my week of emotional turmoil.

Then Monday afternoon, in a moment of rare and absolute stillness (sitting on a sofa in the corner of the classroom having just helped with an afternoon of art projects, waiting for the bell to ring), I had a thought about drinking, followed by a pang. A familiar pang.

'This is a thought, not a craving,' I told myself. And I tried to analyse why it was that the thought had appeared at that moment. I rode it out, but to be honest that sad longing about alcohol has lingered for 2 days now. I think it's starting to drift away, finally.

And there's ***absolutelynofuckingwayI'mactually goingtodrink***.

Just had to make that clear (in bold italics no less).

I'm starting to think that the drinking for me was to fill the silence. I'm having to learn to be still. I'm also having to get to know sad Mrs D. She's there and I never let her out much. Without the heavy, steady alcohol-drinking squashing down my emotions, I am having to learn to ride the waves of emotion naturally when they come. Acknowledge them, feel them, hear them, watch them go.

Is it stupid that I'm only just starting to see now that my heavy alcohol consumption was me choosing to live a life of suppressing emotions? How can you feel, really feel, clearly and simply and in a real way, if you're always pouring booze down your throat? You can't. So I'm having to learn that way of living I guess.

Little did I know when I decided to remove alcohol from my life I was putting myself through an intense life-studies course. Thankfully I've got my fellow students alongside to help with the coursework.

Comment from 'Anonymous'

Good for you! Isn't it amazing when that urge, pang or whatever we call it comes out of nowhere??? It happens to me too. The difference right now is I sit with it, think it through to the last drink instead of only thinking of the first, soothing one. Lord knows it won't just be one. So far so good but it still pisses me off that I can't just have a couple like other people . . . oh well. That's the way it is. Stay strong. Love reading your posts.

I'd be lying if I said it wasn't nice to hear that people are enjoying my posts. Like I've said before—I'll take all the good feelings I can get right now. This really is such an intense process I'm going through. But I'll try and do what this commenter says and stay strong. I need to—because tonight is my 40th birthday party.

I'd really rather not have to host a party, even if it is a combined one with my brother-in-law, and I feel terrible admitting this because I've got lots of friends and family flying in for it. Luckily my brother-in-law is a great guy and also a DJ so he's taking the lead in most of the planning and he's arranged for us to hold the party in a bar near where he works. All I have to do is prepare some nibbles, show up, chat and mingle, maybe dance a bit, not drink alcohol and go home.

Yeah, a fucking doddle.

I'm trying really hard to not feel completely and utterly gutted that I can't just party full-on and have a wild and crazy time. Isn't that what you're supposed to bloody do at a big milestone birthday? Get pissed and talk shit and cruise around and dance and just lark it up? I want to do that! I want to be fun party girl Lotta! That girl I know so well, whose demeanour and attitude I have perfected over years and years.

But I can't. I have to be that slightly uptight edgy sober version of myself that I don't really know well or like much yet.

I've got this thing I do when I have to climb a hill where I just put my head down and charge up as fast as I can to get it over with (not a huge fan of climbing hills). I feel the same way about this party. I just want to put my head down and charge through it and get it over with. I'm not going to drink. No fucking way.

I'm nervous getting ready (I decide to wear something safe and comfortable, including old favourite boots, not taking any bloody fashion risks tonight). I'm nervous driving to the venue. I'm nervous putting out the trays of food and talking with my brother-in-law. I'm very nervous.

Then people start arriving and I find myself doing something extremely odd. I have not planned this at all. This is just what comes out of my mouth, over and over and over as I welcome friends and family into the bar.

'Hey! Great to see you. Have I told you my big news? I've given up alcohol! I can't control it anymore, so I've stopped completely. Welcome to my party!'

I know I'm coming across a bit weird but I can't help myself. I can't pretend it's not the truth. It is the truth, and this is my party and I'll confess if I want to. It calms me down, actually; I'm not pretending anything now. I'm just being what I am which is someone desperately trying to change their ways. Some of my guests are taken aback by my announcement ('How bad were you?' they ask), and I think others find it slightly odd and awkward to be confronted with such sobering news (pun intended). To be perfectly honest I don't care what anyone thinks. I can't afford to. I'm just doing whatever I can to get through the night and not drink.

I float around and chat and mingle but I'm not sure exactly what to do with myself without a drink in my hand (and lots in my belly). My brother-in-law and his mates are having a wild and crazy time on the dance floor, which is great, but my boots, despite being comfortable, aren't made for dancing tonight.

Instead I smoke cigarettes outside on the balcony and try to join in with the loose talk going on out there but I'm struggling a bit to match the party mood. I feel a bit lost and I keep heading to the bar to order Red Bulls. It's certainly not going down in history as the Best Night Ever. But it's fine, and that's good enough for now.

The night is drawing to a close when I find myself sitting at a table with about six good mates and it suddenly dawns on me that we are having a great conversation, a *really* great conversation. None of these people are boozing (Doesn't everyone booze all the time? I'm discovering not) and we all just get chatting and I'm thinking, 'Hell, this is a great chat.' Not loose, raucous, smack talk but a lovely proper conversation about stuff. This conversation is probably the highlight of my night, that and the feeling I have as I drive the car home (full of slurry people singing merrily in the back). I feel incredibly satisfied and proud of myself that

I did it. I made it through my 40th birthday party sober and it was fine!

Sadly, when I climb into bed at 2.30 a.m. I discover I have completely overdone it on the Red Bulls, have over-caffeinated myself and am too wired to sleep. Bugger.

While I may not be hungover the next day, and really pleased with myself for having got through the party sober, I am sleep-deprived and worried whether I did the right thing by announcing my new lifestyle the way I did.

Mrs D Is Going Without (Day 70)

I think I'm going to have to work on getting the tone right when I talk about my removing alcohol from my life.

I don't want to come across as anti-alcohol because in many ways I feel the opposite. Like—'don't let the fun stop just cos I'm not drinking!' (That feeling comes mixed with a bit of me desperately trying to prove that I am still fun without the booze.)

I also don't want to come across holier-than-thou. Like—'you're all dysfunctional drinkers cos I know now that drinking heavily is all about suppressing emotion and how can you really feel when you're pouring wine down your throat constantly, by the way how is that drink there treating you?' Yeah, that's not a good look.

And I want to explain to people that I wasn't exactly vomiting and falling over every night so to that end I'm developing some quick responses to explain what led to my sober lifestyle. 'It was just wine but it was lots of it' and 'Only ever after 5 p.m. but most nights' and 'It wasn't crazy binges just steady heavy drinking' and 'I just got sick of being a boozer'.

Still, despite worrying about how to talk about my not-drinking, I am feeling pretty bloody good about what I'm managing to do. And even if my friends and family don't appreciate how hard it is for me to stay sober, my wonderful blog readers certainly get it.

Comment from 'Nate'
Big deal about your 40th sober—fucking huge deal! Well done—I hope over time everyone sees you as Sober Mrs D and just gets on with it. Normalises it.

Me too, Nate, me too.

16

I'm amazed to realise it's now been just over two months since I had my last binge. That's a decent stint of not-drinking! A good portion of my brain is standing strong and telling me that the world has indeed shifted and my life will never be the same again—that I'm never going back to that boozy nightmare—but there's another part of my brain that is freaking out and lurching all over the show emotionally. Me and my bloody split personality.

Unfortunately, none of my grey matter appears to be communicating with my body. I'm gutted that I don't look any different, I'm not a glowing picture of robust health and I haven't lost any weight. You'd think I'd have lost some bloody weight, given all the calories that are supposedly in wine, wouldn't you?

I'm still dragging myself to the gym a couple of times a week and forcing myself to do some sort of exercise (not something that comes very easily to me). I have formed a nice new routine of stopping at the store opposite the gym on my way home to get some treat-y supplies. Sober treats. And I refuse to feel guilty about them because of the money I'm saving on wine. Sober treats = fresh flowers, magazines, scented candles, nice soaps, face packs, gourmet cheeses, olives, tasty nuts, crackers, all manner of non-alcoholic drinks and lots of varieties of tea.

I'm a bit surprised, actually, at my growing attraction to flavoured green teas. I'm guzzling them daily like some sort of crazy hippy. My big mugs of milky instant coffee are a thing of the past and I'm now starting and finishing every day with a mug of green tea instead. It's really easy to drink and makes me feel good.

No alcohol, herbal tea, good sleep, still exercising—you see why I'm pissed off about not looking any different?

Right by the store is a church hall and I'm fairly certain it's used for AA meetings. I stare at it whenever I drive by and wonder what it would be like to walk into a meeting. The thought freaks me out to be honest; I get nerves in my tummy imagining it. I know that's stupid. I know everyone who goes there would be super-lovely towards me if I showed up, but I just can't imagine doing it. Maybe I'm thinking my drinking wasn't bad enough? Nah, I know they wouldn't judge me on 'how bad' I was. Maybe I'm thinking I don't want strangers climbing into my life? Maybe I'm just chicken-shit? I look up the meeting times online but I never go.

It is stupid, though, because I'm longing for face-to-face contact with other ex-boozers. I would love to be able to look someone in the eye who knows exactly what I'm going through, who can relate to what I'm experiencing. My friends and family are being really kind about my not-drinking, but they can't relate no matter how much they try. I'm pretty sure they don't realise the extent of what I'm going through in trying to live without alcohol: the internal struggles I have at social functions or when I feel some shitty emotion (or frankly on any random weekday at 5 p.m.).

I'm now openly telling people about my big life change. After my slow start at letting out the news (telling another family member or friend every few days), and my strange self-outing at my 40th birthday, I'm comfortable now to say the words more freely. If it feels natural I'll come out with, 'I'm not drinking alcohol anymore', and usually follow up with the blunt truth, 'I've stopped because I can't control it'. I get a few raised eyebrows and shocked reactions but laying it out so boldly works well to distill any misconceptions most of the time (I think it does, anyway). I'm owning the news, it's my story and I'll tell it how I want to. I can't stop anyone gossiping behind my back, but at least I can front-foot it with the truth. For some strange reason I'm not embarrassed by the truth. Alcohol is bloody addictive, for goodness sake; I'm not ashamed that I got addicted to something that is addictive!

Telling everyone in my 'real' life about my blog would, of course, be one easy way for me to reveal more about what I'm going through. I do have a bunch of lovely friends around me in my neighbourhood and lots of friends and family that I'm in regular contact with around the country, but I can't bring myself to tell them about my blog yet. I'm not nervous about what they'll think of it (I'm sure they'll all be interested, impressed and supportive) but I'm nervous about what impact it'll have on the vibe of my online life. I can't bear the thought of my blog losing any of its awesomeness. What if telling people prevents me from being so raw and honest online? What if I lost my precious outlet? What if I retreat back into my head and go back to drinking? I don't want to risk the blog losing its power. It's my main tool and I need it too much.

I'm telling friends that I'm reading sober blogs but I never let on that I'm writing one myself. *Mrs D Is Going Without* is just too unbelievably important and precious to me. It's my special, safe, private place where I can vent, ponder and explore my feelings freely and openly. None of my blog readers know who I really am, they only know me as Mrs D and that anonymity is incredibly comforting and powerful.

Also, without AA or any face-to-face contact with other former boozers, my online community is vitally important.

They know what I'm going through. They're my amazing, wonderful, wise, warm, faceless support group. And there's no-holds-barred on what we discuss.

Comment from 'Sunny'

Why won't you go to AA? Step 1—Admitted we were powerless over alcohol and our lives had become unmanageable. Good luck to you doing it by yourself, but my experience was that I could not do it on willpower alone. By myself I was powerless. I had to go to meetings. I love my meetings and I love the people I have met there. After I went to my first meeting the compulsion left me immediately.

Comment from 'Anonymous'

AA works for some, not for all. I believe I'm in power—I don't like the idea of giving up the power to anyone else. The decisions and choices I make always ultimately come back to me ... There's nothing wrong with reaching out for support and camaraderie but I will never let anyone else be in charge of my sobriety—that's for me to do.

Comment from 'Anonymous'

I am also a non-AA person. It has nothing to do with willpower for me. Instead, it comes from needing to understand myself and what 'I' need to keep sober, not what someone else feels I should have or be doing. I do this by reading from a lot of different sources (AA, Women For Sobriety, blogs, books). I really feel I'm getting to choose what works best for me from all these sources and it *has* been working. I am not 'white-knuckling' it, but my eyes are also open that there will be obstacles down the road that will try to veer me off-course. Blogs like yours help remind me there are others that feel the same way.

My eyes are wide open, too. I might not be reading AA literature, following the Twelve Steps or attending meetings, but I am soaking up information wherever else I can. The journalist and the academic in me just wants to research like crazy. It's that busy brain of mine that needs constant stimulation. I can't help myself, I'm like a huge sponge when it comes to all matters recovery related. I am still working on my Master's thesis part-time (now in the data-gathering stage, carrying out interviews and transcribing them), but it often feels like I'm also doing a completely separate thesis all about sobriety.

If I go to the library website and plug in search terms like 'alcohol' or 'sober' I get directed to books like *The Thinking Person's Guide to Sobriety* by Bert Pluymen; *Still Waters: Sobriety, Atonement, and Unfolding Enlightenment* by William Alexander; John R's *Big Book Unplugged: A Young Person's*

Guide to Alcoholics Anonymous. I get them and I read them and sometimes they help and sometimes they annoy. Usually there's a little nugget of something I gain from each one.

I've also grabbed random books like *Unhooked: How to Quit Anything* by Dr Frederick Woolverton and Susan Shapiro; *From Chocolate to Morphine* by Andrew Weil; and *iWant: My Journey From Addiction and Overconsumption to a Simpler, Honest Life* by Jane Velez-Mitchell.

The two books I'm most enjoying are Jason Vale's *Kick the Drink . . . Easily* and Allen Carr's *The Easy Way To Stop Drinking.* Both of them are really positively influencing my thinking.

I can't get enough of memoirs written by former boozers and addicts. Already I've read books by Augusten Burroughs, Sacha Scobilic, Rob Lowe, Mackenzie Phillips, Steven Tyler, Tom Sykes, Caroline Knapp, Clarissa Dickson-Wright and Jane Lynch.

In addition to all this reading I will often climb into bed with the laptop and watch endless clips on YouTube of former addicts and addiction specialists, and clips of TV programmes like *Intervention* and *Celebrity Rehab.*

And on top of all this I am, of course, reading and commenting on heaps of other sober blogs.

I'm so immersed in the world of alcohol addiction, I'm adopting the lingo. Words like sobriety, recovery and journey are tripping off my tongue (and onto my keyboard) with gay abandon. I am familiar with how pink clouds and relapses usually play out. I know that AA is a fellowship for drinkers and Al-Anon is a fellowship for drinkers' friends and family. I know that NA stands for Narcotics Anonymous. I know that a 'normie' is someone who can drink normally; that is, have one beer and leave it at that or walk away from a restaurant table with wine still in their glass (shock!). I know that a 'dry drunk' is someone who is considered to be 'white-knuckling' their way through the days, not exploring the reasons why they drank, just trying like hell not to do it anymore. My online buddies all seem to be jealous of normies and scathing of dry drunks and I get where they're coming from.

I am not a dry drunk. I am exploring. I am researching. I am navel-gazing. I am fully 'going there' trying to properly analyse my drinking. Why did I booze and how can I now best not-booze? This is key for me: I am determined that I will not face the rest of my life feeling miserable about not-drinking. It is as equal a determination as never returning to being a boozer. I don't want to miserably booze, and I don't want to miserably not-booze. I want to be happy *and* sober. It must be possible to do that. Is it possible to do that?

There's a passage in one of the books I'm reading that really jumps out at me so I type it up into my blog. It's from the book *From Chocolate To Morphine: Everything you need to know about mind-altering drugs* and the authors, Winifred Rosen and Andrew Weil, MD, write:

We think that addiction is a basic human problem whose roots go very deep. Most of us have at some point been wounded, no matter what kind of family we grew up in or what kind of society we live in. We long for a sense of completeness and wholeness and whatever satisfaction we gain from drugs, food, sex, money, and other 'sources' of pleasure really comes from inside of us. That is, we project our power onto external substances and activities, allowing them to make us feel better temporarily. This is a very strange sort of magic. We give away our power in exchange for a transient sense of wholeness, then suffer because the object of our craving seems to control us. Addiction can be cured only when we consciously experience this process, reclaim our power, and recognise that our wounds must be healed from within.

I like this passage. I feel like it's telling me that what I'm trying to do can be done. It's telling me that I have the power within myself to feel content and whole. It's telling me that shit happens to everyone; some of us reach for substances to make us feel better but the substances don't work. They might work temporarily but they don't properly work (and they can bite you on the bum if you get addicted). So this is what I need to do. The substance has gone; now I have to reclaim the power to manage my feelings myself.

17

Reclaim the power to manage feelings myself. Easier said than bloody done.

Mrs D Is Going Without (Day 76)

I hate to say this and be all boring and low and flat and introspective but this weekend has felt really colourless and frankly quite hard work. I just keep thinking that I am the most boring person in the world and everyone else is having way more fun than me and they're going to always have a better life because they can relax with a drink or two or even get a bit naughty and have 4 or 5 and I'm just going to be a boring sober uptight person. I just feel pissed off, that it's not fair and no one is making me do this. In fact no one ever told me I had to stop drinking, it was only me telling myself. And now this weekend I've been telling myself that it's a really kill-joy idea.

Okay, fuck. This is miserably not-boozing and I cannot do this for the next 40 years.

Comment from 'Nate'

There's heaps out there about this feeling you are living— it is a curious mix of loss, mourning and jealousy. There ain't much we can do about it, I've spent hours trying to rationalise a way that I could drink and be normal and the fact is that I just can't. Drink, that is. So just remember drinking as that friend you used to know. And stay strong so we can all be proud of each other!

I do feel that I'm moving in the right direction. Reading and watching everything that I am and slowly adding to the number of days since I last drank is all having some effect. I now know for certain that I do not like to be overly emotional and that drinking helped me to avoid that. It's good to have that basic knowledge about myself. But I've still got a lot to learn. Starting with, how to just be around at home without my beloved wine.

Why did I do so much drinking at home? I used to say quite a lot that I was 'bored', and that drinking wine helped with the 'boredom that comes from being at home with kids all the time'. In a twisted way I thought wine was a clever solution to stop me from getting bored at home 'like all housewives do'. But now I'm wondering if there was more to it than that.

Once again a TV guru helps me, although this time it's not Oprah but the rather slick addiction-specialist Dr Drew. I'm watching *Celebrity Rehab* one afternoon when one of the addicts on the show, in a counselling session, tells Dr Drew that he uses drugs 'cos I'm bored all the time'. Dr Drew quickly interjects with, 'You know boredom is just another word for depression, don't you?'

My mind does that freak-out thing again and goes deathly quiet. I pause the telly. Really? People who say they use drugs or drink to escape boredom are actually depressed? I used to say all the time that I drank because I was bored.

I have to think about this.

Okay, I'm not depressed, I know that. I've had brief black periods in my life and I know what it's like to have that awful feeling that there is nothing worth living for. I don't have that now. I am not depressed. But Dr Drew gets me thinking, on top of the thinking the book *From Chocolate to Morphine* was already getting me to do.

Maybe boredom is the 'basic human problem' that the book spoke of, this longing we have 'for a sense of completeness and wholeness'? Maybe the empty space that I've been calling boredom and filling with wine is actually a normal symptom of the human condition and I just have to live with it? Maybe I have to learn how to just 'be' in the empty space and feel okay? Or is the empty space I've been calling boredom actually the sign there's a problem with me;

particularly, that I've a hole to fill inside me? Dr Drew seems to be implying that it is, so therefore do I need to work on fixing that hole so I can feel whole? Do I even have an empty space? Or am I just normal? Am I actually depressed? Or do I just need to find the power within?

Aaarrrgghhh! For someone who doesn't like navel-gazing this is far too much navel-gazing! All I know for certain is that, where there used to be a fucking shitload of wine, now there's none and it's going to take a hell of a lot of adjusting to that fact.

One thing I am noticing is that this introspection (which I have always scathingly referred to as navel-gazing) is having *shock horror* a positive impact on me. I'm getting a little calmer and slower in my thinking. These are such ginormous questions that I'm asking—about all of life and all of human kind, actually—and I know there aren't going to be any quick solutions. So mentally I'm slowing down and settling a little. Figuring out what's going on inside me is something I can take my time with. There's no big hurry. All I have to do is concentrate on not-drinking and keep heading for the ultimate goal—which is pure unadulterated sober nirvana, of course! One thing I am now certain of is that my heavy drinking was sucking up heaps of my time and energy and stopping me from figuring myself (and life) out.

Of course, in addition to all of this deep thinking I'm still continuing with the mundane stuff of everyday life: cooking meals and filling lunch boxes and cleaning the bathroom and driving to the gym and organising thesis interviews and buying groceries and folding yet another load of washing and watching *Keeping Up with the Kardashians* and chatting with teachers and shopkeepers and neighbours and turning Bruno Mars up loud and 'Should we have roast chicken for dinner tonight?' and 'How did you manage to lose your shoes?' and 'That was a great interview this morning, honey' and through all of this I discover that sometimes all I need is for some time to pass and things smooth out by themselves.

Mrs D Is Going Without (Day 82)

Feeling much better, have got through my 'hard done by' phase and have quietly settled back into 'this is just the way it has to be' mode. Drove to a trendy bar during the week to interview someone for my thesis and actually imagined myself buying a shiny glass of chardonnay and sipping it and the thought wasn't at all nice. I so, so, so, don't want to drink.

Being in the bar for my thesis interview was interesting. My interviewee and I sat in a quiet corner inside so I could record our conversation on a dictaphone, and right outside our window in the courtyard was a large group of people drinking and laughing together. Alcohol seemed crucial to the scene. It made me feel a little sad but also pissed off.

Why should alcohol have all the power to make that scene fun? I left the bar hyper-aware of the hard mental work I still need to do. I've got to shift my thinking so that I don't feel miserable every time other people are drinking. This is different to the figuring-out-what-to-do-with-the-uncomfortable-empty-space I (maybe) need to do. This is about the how-to-not-be-a-miserable-non-boozer-around-others goal that I have.

I go back to my books. Jason Vale's *Kick the Drink . . . Easily* and Allen Carr's *The Easy Way To Stop Drinking* are the key books for this. I keep renewing them at the library so I can read them nice and slowly. Both Vale and Carr are really getting inside my brain. They both espouse the sort of attitude that I really, really, really want to have; that living without alcohol is not about living a life feeling deprived and miserable, but about living feeling happy and free. I have to believe this, or I will be a miserable non-boozer forevermore.

Both of these dudes firmly believe we've all been brain-washed since birth into believing a whole bunch of things about alcohol that are just not true. Allen Carr summarises it like this:

From the moment we are born, our young brains are bombarded daily with information telling us that alcohol quenches our thirst, tastes good, makes us happy, steadies our nerves, gives us confidence and courage, removes our inhibitions, relieves boredom and stress, eases pain, helps us to relax, and releases the imagination. At the same time it is an absolute essential for successful social interaction.

Well, yeah, that is what I've always believed. Until the stuff bloody turned on me. Or was it against me from the start? I didn't used to think it was, I always thought alcohol made things better, more fun, more bearable, etc. That is until recently when clearly it didn't. So, did it ever? Hmmm, now these guys have got me wondering. Jason Vale puts it pretty bluntly:

The truth is that alcohol does the opposite of what it appears to do. It causes mental and physical stress, mental and physical tension, mental and physical aggravation. It suppresses your nervous system, destroys your courage, undermines your confidence and keeps you a slave to the stuff.

Both Vale and Carr are so passionate and fired up that I'm finding it pretty easy to be swept along by their arguments. It probably helps that they're both using very direct and persuasive language. Lots of 'do you really want to spend the rest of your life waiting for the next dose of poison?' No, Allen Carr, I don't! And 'you will have more courage and confidence and, far from having a void in your life when you stop, you will feel more fulfilled than you have in years'. Show me how, Jason Vale, show me how!

Piece by piece, chapter by chapter, and with great conviction, both Carr and Vale systematically break down all of the commonly held beliefs about what alcohol offers and exposes them as fallacies. They say alcohol doesn't quench our thirst (it's a diuretic and actually dehydrates), it doesn't taste good (it tastes like poison and we simply get used to and tolerate the foul taste in order to get the drug into our bodies), it doesn't make us happy (it deprives us of our natural senses and numbs genuine feelings, creating a false sense of pleasure), it doesn't steady our nerves (it slurs our speech and dulls our sense of taste and smell), it's not good for us (it breaks down our immune systems, making us less resistant to diseases), it doesn't give us courage (it removes our natural fears and gives us a false sense of confidence that makes us unprotected and vulnerable), it doesn't remove our inhibitions (it obliterates all the checkpoints between our brain and our mouth), it doesn't relieve boredom (it stupefies and alters your perspective), it doesn't relieve stress (it creates more stress because every time you drink you are physically, mentally, emotionally, socially and financially worse off), it doesn't ease pain (it causes low blood sugar, drains the body of water, overworks the liver, pancreas and kidneys, and leaches oxygen from the brain), it doesn't help us relax (it gives an instant rush of glucose to the bloodstream, stimulating excess production of insulin), it doesn't release the imagination (it destroys our brain cells and memories), and finally it isn't essential for successful social interactions (being sociable means being friendly, companionable and interacting with others, and if you are doing this without consuming alcohol, you are still being sociable).

Phew. These arguments are spun out in great detail across many, many pages. It's a lot to get my head around. But it's incredibly satisfying to read and makes me feel a whole lot better about my decision. Well, of course it does because I'm at the point where I can't touch the bloody stuff without the wheels falling off my life. But even so, even with this brutal truth about me and alcohol not being able to mix, what they say seems to make perfect sense.

But what am I supposed to do? Convince everyone else in the whole wide world that everything we think about alcohol is a crock of shit? No. I have to live in a world awash with alcohol and just be happy myself without it.

The bit about alcohol not being necessary for social situations is the bit I'm latching on to the most. I really want to believe that alcohol is not the all-powerful elixir that makes socialising fun. And to this end Jason Vale has some encouraging words:

It is never the drink that is making you happy, it is the occasions when you drink it and the people you are with.

When people are at an exciting party with fun friends, they will be happy. This is because it is a happy occasion. It's not the alcohol that determines whether you have a good evening but the company, the banter and the social aspect of being out with friends combined with the music and the dancing, but never the alcohol.

And then he slams me with this:

Remember you stop drinking, not living. Once the poison has left your mind and body completely, it will not matter if it's New Year, your birthday or a holiday as you simply will not miss drink. You will be able to celebrate just like you used to with dancing, good company, fireworks, good friends, laughter, having a blast. The difference will be that you will remember the entire evening and will wake up feeling refreshed and alive. The added bonus will be that you will always be able to drive yourself home.

This is where I want to get to. This is how I want to be.

18

Reading Carr and Vale has me primed to get my grey matter working. They've given me a lot to go on. As normal life continues on—Corin busy at work, the boys just consistently busy and me keeping everything running as smoothly as possible—I practise my new thinking. I practise it in the shower in the morning, I practise it as I'm driving in the car, I practise it when I'm lumbering around in a gym class, and of course I practise it in my blog.

Mrs D Is Going Without (Day 84)

I know there will be times when I do have a sad pang about not drinking but I also know that those times will pass and the majority of my time will be spent feeling amazing without booze clouding the way.

I also know that everything is just as fun and great without alcohol. A cafe table beside the water with the sun shining, a platter of nibbles and a shiny drink and laughter is just as fun if the drink is a lime and soda.

A great party is a great party because it's a great party, not because I'm getting hammered. A boring party will always be a boring party no matter how much I drink.

A celebratory toast is loving and cheerful because that's what a celebratory toast with other humans is. It is not given its currency because it involves then sipping a drink that (for me) triggers a switch in your brain that turns you into a loser lush.

Stress isn't going to go away with 6 glasses of wine, it's just going to hide behind the door until you've sobered up then jump out at ya—'Still here! Now deal with me with that hangover and the guilts.' Same goes for Sadness, Anger, Hurt and Grief.

In fact in my house those emotions had a secret room behind the door and they used to have a private party in there while they waited for me to sober up. They'd plot their next move: 'Let's get her at 3 a.m. when she gets up to go to the loo and keep her up for the rest of the night, yeah!'

They live with me constantly now, those emotions, no hiding and plotting, and I'm getting used to having them around. It's okay, you know. It's okay.

The more I write posts on my blog, the more I become aware that putting my thoughts into words is how I work things out.

Talking aloud, writing, using language, is a vital part of my process. The added bonus (now that people are reading my blog) is that in writing to myself I appear to also be helping others. This is another completely unexpected development surrounding my blog.

Comment from 'Anonymous'

Great post! You are absolutely right. I am going to print this one. I am going to keep reading it until I don't have to anymore.

Great blog. Keep writing.

Comment from 'Anonymous'

I totally agree with the comment above ... great post!!! I LOVE your way with words ... I'm keeping this one ... Loser Lush!!!! OMG, you are the best!!! Thank you again for this blog!!!

Okay, it does still feel a little weird that I am getting thanks for blogging from random people through the internet. I initiated the blog to help myself. But the thanks I'm getting for sharing stuff I'm going through is super-cool. It makes me feel really good and, as I've said before, I'll take all the good feelings I can get right now. This is a huge turnaround in my thinking that I am attempting here. I have spent twenty-plus years believing alcohol to be the source of all fun. Parties were for getting rip-snorted, I thought. Weddings were for cutting loose, I thought. Friday nights were for drinking more than usual, I thought. And of course 5 o'clock was wine o'clock, I thought.

Mrs D Is Going Without (Day 86)

A large part of my identity for twenty-odd years has been 'fun, naughty Mrs D', that fun, naughty, chatty, up-for-it party girl. I don't want to see her go! But now I'm sober. So how do I keep bringing her to the party? I haven't worked that out yet. Because if fun, naughty Mrs D is all about the booze then she's gone forever. But if I can be that way sober then great. Thing is, I don't know if I can. It's different being out if you're not boozing. Cos ... well ... you're not boozing. I had fun at my 40th but I felt sober. Very, very sober. A sober life is ... very, very sober. So it will be a different life and maybe I'll carve out a new self-image, or adapt the old one. It's early days, I can't tell how that's going to go.

I do hope I like the new sober me as she emerges. Because if I don't, I might be tempted to go back to the boozy me I know so well.

Comment from 'Tina Mary'

Most sober people I know have found a new person inside—infinitely superior to the drunken persona.

It takes time, but believe me, that person is inside you, and what an adventure to find her!

Comment from 'Nate'

Don't be scared of being sober you.

It might be that your beautiful personality is finally getting some sunshine and it is 'peeking out from behind the barricades' of your old drinking self.

You will soon be a funny, entertaining bastard again once you grow back into yourself, without the false rollercoaster of alcohol.

Keep going, there is no destination, just the rolling hills of the journey . . .

See how the recovery lingo is tripping off everyone's keyboard in the online blogging world? I still can't believe how little I knew about what I was getting into when I decided to take the booze away. This path that I am on is totally unexpected and fascinating. I'm on a journey, baby! And it is a journey, a journey of discovery. All of the clichés are true.

I have to be honest: despite my discomfort with the moods and the low phases and the awkward feeling I've sometimes had when socialising, overall I'm really enjoying this process. It might be partly due to the fun I'm having with my blog and the lovely, warm online community I'm now a part of, but I also think that it's just so goddamn interesting learning about all this stuff. I'm endlessly fascinated. I'm discovering a whole new area of interest that I've previously been completely closed off to. I'm gobsmacked at the millions of people who are wrestling with and writing about all this recovery stuff. I've thrown myself into this arena and I'm really digging it.

One of the many things I've learned through all of my reading and research is that reaching 90 days sober is a big deal. And yay for me, I'm almost there. It seems to be used as a bit of a 'celebration point' in many fellowships and organisations, the thought being that if you've made it to 90 days without drinking (or using drugs) you've got a good strong foothold in sobriety.

A good strong foothold in sobriety—I like this. I like this a lot. I'm clinging to this, actually. As I draw closer to this magical mystical number of days without wine, I'm getting quite excited. Ninety days feels like a big important sign that I can actually do this. I'm feeling quietly jazzed and proud of myself.

I want to do something to mark the occasion but am in a bit of a tizz about what that should be. I know from reading other sober blogs that if I was going to meetings I'd be getting a special chip and a big round of applause to mark the occasion. Other ex-boozers understand what a big deal 90 days is. Unfortunately the people I have around me don't. I'm sure my family and friends would rally around if I made a song and dance; they'd probably even gather in our living room and give me a big round of applause if I asked nicely, but that's not going to happen. I'll have to organise myself a little private party instead.

Mrs D Is Going Without (Day 89)

I've been getting excited about tomorrow and feel like I should do something special like make a big pavlova! And cover it with whipped cream and fresh berries and a broken-up Flake bar. Lots of lovely crumbs of chocolate. That would be a statement.

But personally, inside me, I have to say that the journey to this point has been intense and revealing. And now that I'm here I feel a certain level of calm about living a life without alcohol.

Having said that, I did have a pang or two yesterday, accompanied by a small stomach turn (nerves?) and a kind of incredulous voice inside saying, 'Really? Never again? Really?' I think it's still going to be hard, and at times I'll be sad that I can't be a casual drinker.

But I can't, so there, move on Mrs D.

The pangs are still coming at me. A sad little thought here or a nervy feeling in my tummy there. I feel them, and they hurt, they really do, an actual physical pain sometimes. Just a total fucking bummer of a painful thought that I can't ever drink again. I try really hard to push these painful thoughts aside as quickly as I can. I refuse to let a little pang turn into a big wall of words trying to convince me to drink. I feel the pain but I keep reminding myself that I just can't drink alcohol ever again. I make myself think back to the horrible boozy person I was; the embarrassing sloppy behaviour, the miserable 3 a.m. guilt. And I desperately cling to a mental image of the person I want to be—sober and together and calm and wise and groomed and leggy and . . . okay, enough, I doubt I'm ever going to be uber-groomed and no amount of thinking is going to make my legs longer! I'll just work on picturing myself as the nice sober person I want to be.

Comment from 'Sober With Faith'

In NA the 90 day chip is red, and for a good reason. It's a chip of warning. It's at this time that we start to feel good about ourselves, physically have detoxed, and mentally feel more acutely alive. It's a time when some of us think maybe a drink is not so bad. Keep up the good work. You sound like you are doing really well.

Once again my online community is filling in the gaps for me; lovely comments offering support and wisdom trickle in after I write each post. I so appreciate all of it and soak it all up. I'm often reminded by people—like Sober With Faith—not to get complacent. The message I keep hearing is, don't assume you're 'fixed', never assume you can start drinking again and will be able to moderate next time. I won't be able to. Once a boozer always a boozer. This is good to hear right now, given I am feeling self-satisfied and proud of my 90 days. (Note to self: Don't Get Complacent.) Now, celebration time!!!!!

Mrs D Is Going Without (Day 90)

90 Days Hurray!

90 Days Hurray!

Hi Ho the Dairy-O,

90 Days Hurray!

What a lovely 90th day of sobriety I had. What a contrast the day was compared with my last binge which also fell on a Monday.

Yesterday I went to the gym, went and bought Mr D and I a new bed! (this wasn't on a whim, our old one is one I bought before I even met him), made some fresh ginger beer (thanks Jamie Oliver), ginger crunch and a pavlova while the Little Guy was napping, had a lovely family dinner then pottered round cleaning up the house while Mr D took our two eldest to their Scouts meeting. Bathed the Little Guy then made train tracks with him. We all gorged on pavlova when the others got home, then put the kids to bed, lay on the sofa watching TV and ... *filed my nails!!!* Yes, ladies and gentlemen ... some personal grooming!!!

Actually some weird changes are occurring in my newfound sober life. I file my nails more often. I'm thinking I might start *shock horror* flossing my teeth every night. I have plucked my eyebrows more often (I once did this pissed on the sofa in the half-dark and the result was disastrous). The first thing I now put in my tummy every morning is a cup of green tea. What am I, some sort of crazy hippy?! I used to start every day with a huge mug of milky instant coffee but now it's green tea and it really makes me feel much cleaner and lighter.

Cleaner and lighter. That would sum up my feeling in general at this point of 90 days. Cleaner and lighter with no guilt or hangovers, clean teeth, neat nails and semi-shaped eyebrows. But not resting on my laurels. Someone told me yesterday that the 90-day chip is red to warn against being complacent. That was great to hear. I'm considering myself warned. So am going to keep up my inner work and continue to work on training my brain to accept a life with no alcohol added.

19

I may not get a round of applause on my 90th sober day but I get lots of virtual claps and hugs in the form of comments on my blog and that is more than enough for me. It's totally fun celebrating a sober milestone but it does get me thinking about what I'm doing and how I'm labelling myself.

Here I am, embracing a traditional milestone marked in fellowship ceremonies all over the world, accepting fully that I have a problem with alcohol and can never touch it again, yet I am still steadfastly refusing to call myself the 'A' word. I'm not hiding my problem, I'm telling people left, right and centre that I've stopped drinking because I can't control it, but I have never, ever called myself an alcoholic. I don't consider myself an alcoholic. I am not an alcoholic.

Mrs D Is Going Without (Day 92)

Hi, my name is Mrs D and I am a . . . *coughs* . . . um . . .
hi. I'm Mrs D and . . . um . . . huh . . . *clears throat* . . .
sorry, let's try that again. Hi. I'm Mrs D. And I. Am. A . . .
. . . . . . dysfunctional drinker.

I like to call myself a dysfunctional drinker. A boozer.
An enthusiastic wine-drinker. But alcoholic, no. Semantics?
Probably. But still. I don't want to call myself an alcoholic.
For one thing I think it provides too blunt a label, or at
least one that I'm not comfortable with. But also . . . well
. . . I dunno . . . I'm embarrassed to say that I am one. It
conjures up images of derelict losers and I'm not one of
'them'. You know the type. Those winos in the gutter.
Those smelly ladies with filthy clothes and unkempt
hair I see in my supermarket with trolleys filled with big
casks of wine.

I mean, I never drank cask wine! Admittedly my
bottles were only worth about $10 but, you know, there
was glass involved. No cardboard round here. And I wasn't
a stumbling drunk out on the streets creating a scene.
Okay, so there was that one time I sort of stumbled in
front of my in-laws while holding our 6-year-old and sort
of dropped him a bit . . . but I don't think they all knew
how much wine I'd poured into myself that evening. Oh
and there's those favourite earrings that I lost during
almighty binges (still think they might have gone down

the drain, there was vomiting involved). So that's all pretty sloppy behaviour. Me as a derelict loser, yeah.

Allen Carr says the definition of an alcoholic is someone who has lost control over their intake. Well, I had definitely lost control over my intake. I think I lost it back in the late 1980s actually. But, sorry Allen, I'm not ready to own that label yet.

My sober buddies online don't like this, and make their feelings clear with their comments on my blog.

Comment from 'Nate'

Be an alcoholic, that's just what we are, it's a badge of honour to say you do things 'thoroughly and to exhaustion' in a way.

It's sort of revolting to accept you have a label that you have always reviled, but we are much more than just one label.

Comment from 'Recovery Jane'

Labels only hold the weight you allow them to. In the beginning I couldn't handle the alcoholic label but once I was defeated I could. Simply because I began to see how it fit. Don't label yourself if you don't want to but don't allow the lack of a label to grey that line in the sand you've drawn.

Comment from 'Anonymous'

Until I really admitted to myself that I was/am an alcoholic I couldn't give up. And if I had managed to give up without that admission I could have remained in denial, secretly convincing myself that I wasn't really. Just had to cut down a bit ... etc., etc. Really just setting myself up for a relapse.

I'm not exactly feeling the online sober love on this one. Whatever. Don't care. I am not an alcoholic. I am a dysfunctional drinker who couldn't control it and had to take it away and is now learning how to live without it. I'm not going to label myself an alcoholic and I'm not going to let that lack of a label stop me from forging ahead with my goal of learning how to live happily without alcohol.

Live *happily* without alcohol. It has to be *happily*. I can't bear the thought of being a miserable sober git for the rest of my life. I have to be able to go out and genuinely enjoy myself, not feel like I'm missing out and pretending to have a good time. So far my sober social forays haven't been entirely successful on this front. I've struggled a bit, forced smiles onto my face and done weird things like fetching alcohol for others or overindulging on energy drinks. Fashion failures haven't helped, either. I'm determined there will be no more inside-out clothing, shoes that don't fit or skirts that restrict movement. And I am determined that I won't feel edgy and wound-up all the time.

Lucky me, I've got plenty of opportunities ahead to practise my new sober socialising techniques (just a little bit of sarcasm there). The silly season is upon us, and not only do we have a bunch of Christmas parties to attend, but we're also hosting a big family group at our house for four days. Excellent.

I gird my sober loins and plunge headfirst into a busy weekend of parties. Friday afternoon we take the kids along to a *Breakfast* team barbecue at Corin's colleagues' house. I've met most of his workmates already but I do feel nervous as we pull up to the house, which is annoying. I'm not usually shy. But then again I'd usually be gratefully accepting a nice big glass of wine pretty soon after walking in the door. Not being able to do that has got me off-kilter (to say the least).

I feel like I've totally flipped my world upside-down, to be brutally honest.

Walking down the long driveway toward the house, I try to work my brain with my new techniques. 'What does this social event offer?' I ask myself. 'This is about Corin's team celebrating the end of a busy year, summer arriving and Christmas being around the corner. This barbecue is about congratulating a colleague who has a wedding coming up, the kids having a fun time with the pool and lots of yummy food. This is not about me and whether I'm drinking or not.'

I feel like bursting in the door, shouting *'Here comes a whole new me!'*, but I don't, of course. Instead I slope in nervously, smile and say hi to people, dart my eyes around to see what drinks are out, and try to chat without sounding unnatural.

The hostess asks me what I'd like to drink and when I answer my voice comes out a bit shaky. What the fuck? I almost want to slap myself. This isn't normal. But then what is normal for me nowadays? My old normal response would have been a chirpy 'Oohh . . . a wine thanks!' but my new normal is a wobbly 'Lemonade please'. She doesn't know me at all so doesn't bat an eye. Maybe she thinks I'm not really much of a drinker. Ha! If only she knew the truth.

Time passes. I chat a bit. ('I'm working on my Master's thesis.') Admire the new house. ('Fabulous walk-in wardrobe.') Help the kids into their togs. ('Don't worry, it's not that deep.') Calm the kids down when they freak out about how deep it is. ('Just sit here with me for a while.') Admire the whole baked fish and the chocolate fountain. ('Gourmet delights!') And there comes a point where I realise I'm relaxed. No one else gives a shit that I'm not drinking alcohol and even I begin to feel like I don't give a shit. Just before the meal is served I'm standing on the deck talking to a new workmate of Corin's and we're having a laugh and I have this shocking little realisation that I'm not bothered that the glass I'm holding has lemonade in it. When we all sit down for lunch and speeches are being made for the groom-to-be, I'm stoked for him but mostly I'm just so stoked for myself that I'm actually doing this barbecue sober and it's fine!

I'm ridiculously happy driving home and getting into bed later on.

Saturday morning I wake up feeling bright and oh-so-proud of myself. Most of the day is spent taking the kids to a Christmas party that TVNZ throws for the children of all staff. I'm happy amid the noisy madness, moving around fetching food, clutching balloon creations and helping the kids on and off the bouncy castle. Last year I was at this same party with a raging hangover after writing myself off completely at a concert the night before (this was the night I fell over backwards for no reason other than that booze had taken my balance away). It's such a blessed relief not to be dealing with this chaos with a pounding head this year.

We're knackered driving home but there's no let-up in this weekend of Christmas party madness. Corin and I now have to get ready to go to yet another TVNZ Christmas function. This one is the big one. The entire News and Current Affairs department is descending on a hip downtown bar for a night of revelry. All the famous on-camera faces will be there, along with all the behind-the-scenes workers, and all their partners.

I wear something safe and black, my sister comes over to babysit, and Corin and I go out for dinner together before hitting the bar. I feel a little edgy but get busy thinking my new sober thoughts, concentrating on what the night ahead has to offer: 'Tonight is about us being out together without kids, about finally eating at the Malaysian restaurant we've been hearing so much about, about checking out a bar that I've heard is super-cool and watching his entire workplace celebrate the end of a busy year. Tonight is not about me and alcohol.'

The Malaysian food is as delicious as all the reviews indicated it would be and, driving to the bar afterwards, again I work my brain to focus on the event ahead and make myself remember the awful sloppy drunk me that's been emerging at parties recently.

We manage to find a carpark a couple of blocks away from the bar. As we walk towards it I can see that it's heaving. My heart starts beating so I cling to Corin's arm and place a smile on my face for our entry.

It's hardly necessary—as soon as we step inside the door we get sucked in and swept up in the party. It's dark and noisy and crowded and immediately I bump into someone I know.

'Lotta!' she cries. 'Long time no see!' She lunges towards me. 'How are you? What are you up to nowadays?' she asks with boozy breath.

'Hey!' I reply. 'Well, actually, funny you should ask.' I take a deep breath and then launch in. 'If you really want to know I've recently made a big decision that I have to stop drinking because I can't control alcohol so I'm learning all these new techniques to help me so that I don't feel like I'm missing out. It's fascinating to start looking at alcohol in a different light and to realise what a fallacy it is and how we're all brainwashed into thinking it makes everything better when it doesn't . . .'

20

No, just joking. As if. I don't think this is the time or place for me to rave on about my quest for blissful sobriety. 'I'm great, thanks!' is what simply comes out of my mouth and I start talking about my thesis research while Corin goes to fetch me a Red Bull from the bar. (I am having just one. I have learnt my lesson about energy drinks.) It does feel good to have a drink in my hand and I tell myself that for all anyone knows it could have vodka in it. I decide to pretend to myself that it is actually vodka and Red Bull and for some reason this private deceit relaxes me. I know no one probably gives a toss what I'm drinking but whatever works for me, right?

There are quite a few people here who I know from my own work at TVNZ over the years and it's fun chatting and catching up. I feel strangely cocooned in the dark party atmosphere and actually quite safe and calm. Some people are obviously drunk, some people aren't. I don't really care. It is what it is. I'm just concentrating on me and as the evening goes on I start to feel quite amazing. This night, this party, this one is a breakthrough. I don't exactly go crazy on the dance floor but then it was never likely to be that sort of party for me, given this isn't my current gang of workmates. I mingle and chat away until about 11 p.m. and then Corin and I decide we've had enough and slip quietly out the back door. I actually feel like I'm bouncing down the footpath as we leave. Yep, there's definitely a geeky spring in my step walking back to the car. I actually did have fun!

And, boy, I could get used to this driving home sober thing. Jason Vale was right. It feels so good getting behind the wheel! All the way home I'm wishing for a drink-driving checkpoint so I can show off how clever I am being.

Mrs D Is Going Without (Day 98)

I'm just going to say this quietly because I don't want to come across as all cocky and confident, and maybe this is another pink cloud floating by in my life (I love the whole pink cloud concept, why are they called pink clouds anyway?) but I just love love love love being sober. I have so much more self-respect. Someone once commented on my blog when I was going to an event and was nervous that I should 'raise a glass of self-respect' instead of booze and I thought that was such a great concept. My self-respect is so much higher now that I'm not feeling so horribly dysfunctional.

And another lovely chap keeps commenting to me to 'be kind to myself' and I love that concept as well because it carries so much weight. It doesn't just say be kind, it says look after, nurture, love, protect. All those things are true when you are being brave and making a big scary, almost unheard of (in my circle of life) decision to live without alcohol.

I feel so much more 'in touch' with myself. This is a hard one to explain but when my brain isn't affected by alcohol so much anymore, I can trust all my feelings and emotions, know that I'm feeling them honestly and fully and not under a cloud. Also I don't have those little memories when they're vague and I think 'was I pissed when I thought that/said that/did that?'

I just feel better. Emotionally and physically. I had a huge weekend with a barbecue on Friday night, two parties on Saturday plus hosting a lunch here on Sunday. Last night Mr D and I got into bed at 7.23 p.m.! and we were absolutely knackered, but I said to him how different it was to feel that exhausted feeling after a busy social weekend but without the headaches, sick guts or guilt.

I actually can't think of a single reason why I would want to go back to wine again. Hope I'm not getting lulled into a false sense of security.

(Incidentally, parties are fine sober until about 11 p.m. when people start giving you sloppy hugs and stop making much sense and at that point slipping out the back door is advisable.)

Sadly my self-satisfied sober joy doesn't last. Monday comes, I'm tired, and at 5 p.m. I start hankering for a wine. Just a few thoughts, not a huge wave of them like it would have been 90-odd days ago when I was first sober, but they're still there. I push the thoughts aside, visualise myself going to bed sober, get through the witching hours and retire early. Tuesday, same thing. This seems to be a pattern for me. I can manage social occasions okay, but in the quiet weekdays I struggle. It's that bloody 'empty space' again. What does that say about me?

I ponder on this as we creep closer to Christmas Day. I've got a lot to do for Christmas this year; we're hosting a four-day extravaganza with ten-plus people descending on our house. I have to borrow mattresses just to fit everyone in. I'm trying to be cool and calm and cruisey and, you know, that low-maintenance version of myself that I so want to be. But with my life having flipped on its head and my brain all raw and sober all the time, I find myself getting really stressed as the day approaches. Can I possibly get through Christmas surrounded by drinkers and not-drink?

If I do, it'll be a big deal. For me, Christmas has always been about food and wine and wine and wine (unless I'm pregnant or breastfeeding). Last Christmas I started with bubbles at breakfast and didn't stop drinking all day. I just kept a steady supply of booze going down my throat from 8 a.m. until about 9 p.m. . . . . I didn't fall over or vomit, but I'm pretty sure I was slurring in the afternoon and certainly would have had a distracted, boozy demeanour going on. We have a framed photo from that day of me and my dad, smiling with our arms around each other. I'm wearing a very expensive blue dress and a lovely brooch. There is a pink paper hat from out of a cracker on my head and I am leaning into Dad. To most people I probably look fine. But I look at it and just see bloated and drunk.

This year (all going well) I won't be blurry and distracted. I won't look bloated in any photos (I've finally started losing weight—woohoo!), and I won't slur my words. But will I be happy? Jury's out on that one.

One thing's for sure, I can't hide away. I can't let the family down and I don't want to be a glum non-drinker, goddamnit! I have to do this and do it sober and act like I'm fine and maybe I will be fine but if not at least I'll come out the other side in one sober piece. Thankfully I've got my awesome blogging tool, my precious outlet, and I claw desperately for it as the 25th draws closer.

Mrs D Is Going Without (Day 107)

My first sober Christmas. I've been looking forward to it actually. A chance to show everyone how happy I am sober. Oh clever sober me! Planning nice fresh ginger beer drinks and lime and mint crushed with ice and soda water. Super! Wonderful! Awesome!

But here I am, four sleeps to go, it's nearly midnight, I'm wound up like a top, my brain is whirring and I've just snuck quietly out of the bedroom to come write this blog in the hope that it will release some of the tension in my thoughts and I can get to sleep.

I think I've been living in a lovely sober bubble for the last however-many days that it's been since I took the wine away. Just me in my house with my lovely husband and sons and my neighbourhood of friends plus family, some close, some far away, all there on the phone and email etc.

And now it's Christmas and everyone is descending on us and I'm doing all the organising (which is fine, I'm an organisational geek) but there's things being said and actions being taken that is the usual stuff of families but it's like brutal fingers are poking, poking, poking at my bubble upsetting my quite delicate equilibrium. I don't think I realised quite how delicate it was.

It doesn't help that I wrote in my last post that I loved 'getting out of it' and I've just been thinking of getting out of it lately. Just getting totally 'out of it'. OUT of it. OUT OF IT. Just getting out of it.

It's not going to happen, though. Oh no siree bob. No fucking way. I'm going to grit my teeth and get through. And who knows, maybe this tension will pass and I'll enjoy myself! I'm sure I will, actually. Once everyone is here in one place I can submit to the craziness and look in my boys' faces and feel good for them and look in the mirror and feel good for myself because all I have to do is not-drink and everything will be alright in the end.

The blogosphere is awash with stressed ex-boozers writing posts just like mine. Sober shoulders are tensing right around the world and we're all devising and sharing our coping strategies online. It's awesome; I don't feel the slightest bit alone in my sober stress, despite my family not really getting what a big deal this is for me. Through the magical entity that is my blog, a community of likeminded people is supporting and fortifying me. The camaraderie that is floating around the internet is priceless.

Comment from 'Sunny'

Good luck Mrs D. Remember, it's the first drink that does the damage. Don't pick up the first one and you won't get drunk. There are no days off if you are an alcoholic.

Comment from 'Milly'

Day 100 for me, and you and me and all of us out here in the sober blogosphere are going to soldier on through this holiday season.

Comment from 'Annabel'

This will be my first sober holiday. I had a meltdown about a week ago where I felt completely overwhelmed with everything I had to do and all the feelings that go along with that. I've never had to actually deal with them before. Things feel better now and I bet you can get to that place too. The one thing that keeps me going is how miserable I was this time last year when I was drinking heavily. That was a very Un-Merry Christmas. Good luck to you!

In the final few days before everyone arrives I get busy organising the house and stocking the cupboards. For the past few weeks we've had emails flying around the family developing a delicious menu. I've received everyone's financial contribution and race around the city picking up special deli products, fresh fruit and vegies, and gourmet meat from the butcher. I have let it be known that I'm not interested in discussing or purchasing the alcohol. It was a little nerve-racking doing this but I'm trying to be brave. I've got no idea what everyone is thinking about my not-drinking. I haven't heard much, other than 'good on you', which is nice. At least no one has tried to convince me to keep drinking. On the flip side, nor are they asking me much about it. It's all largely going unsaid which is . . . I don't know what that is, actually. It just is what it is.

21

I'm very wound up and totally self-obsessed as family members start arriving from around the country. As far as I'm concerned this Christmas is all about me and my new sober lifestyle. I'm so locked in my own head that I'm a bit taken aback to realise my family members aren't also focused on me. Can't they see this first sober Christmas is a huge fucking deal for me? It would appear not; all I'm getting is the odd throwaway comment. I sneak into the bedroom when I can to secretly write a quick post.

Mrs D Is Going Without (Day 110)

Christmas Eve and almost all my family are here. Last night the first big evening together.

I was called 'amazing' . . .

I was called 'virtuous' and 'boring' . . .

And I was warned 'just don't start lecturing anyone else' . . .

As always it feels good to write about what's going on, it almost makes it feel like I become a character in a drama rather than ordinary Lotta trying to stay sober in a house filled with people drinking alcohol. Of course my wonderful blog readers let me know they have my back.

Comment from 'Caroline'
Ooo. Sounds like a tough room. They'll calm down eventually. I promise!

Comment from 'Sunny'
Sounds about as good as it gets! Keep quiet and they'll soon get used to it and stop mentioning it. :-)

I'm trying hard to utilise my new sober-thinking techniques. I'm making myself pause and consider: what does this event offer? And then think through the answers. Okay . . . Christmas . . . it's a time to reconnect with extended family, it's a time to eat beautiful meals, a time to give and receive gifts, a time of great excitement for our kids, a time . . . oh goddam it, this is a hard one . . . Christmas is *such* a time to drink.

I keep sneaking into the bedroom to get on the laptop and read other blogs. Mr SponsorPants has posted an awesome

'Sober Holiday Survival Guide'. It includes great advice like, 'Remember, you don't have to go' (sadly they're all coming to me) and 'Remember, you can leave' (that would be weird and where would I go? The beach? Actually, that's not a bad idea). But by far the best tip he has is, 'Remember, other people find the holidays difficult and emotionally charged as well. You're not the only one having a tough time of it—watch for your ego, and rather than sit in your own upset, see who and how you can help wherever you may be or whomever you may be with.'

Yay for Mr SponsorPants. He's so right. Of course everyone has their own shit going on. Of course it's not all about me. This is the perfect thing for me to hear right now. I mentally slap myself out of my self-obsession and pause to take a look around. Suddenly my eyes are open to all that is going on for my family members. Someone stressed out here, someone struggling there, someone feeling emotional over there. It's great to have my eyes opened like this. I'm not the only one with stuff going on. 'Rather than sit in your own upset, see who and how you can help', Mr SponsorPants said. This is such great advice.

Mrs D Is Going Without (Day 111)

Christmas Day. Man, we are churning through the work. Preparing meals, cleaning up, relaxing for 2 minutes then lurching into the next meal. It's a food and drink feast. A rolling festival of food.

Funny thing is, my non-alcohol beverages seem to be more popular than wine and beer! Everyone is drinking alcohol but they're not really pounding it (like I would be). Maybe it's because I'm not? Still, the main Christmas meal is tonight so perhaps they'll get amongst it then. I've already thought that if that happens, I'll take myself off to bed.

I'm halfway through Christmas Day when I realise I'm feeling fine about not drinking. Jeepers, this is unbelievable!

Comment from 'Milly'
Merry Christmas, Mrs D!

Comment from 'Nate'
Merry Christmas, is nice to be fresh and sober for the first time in decades!

Comment from 'Lacey'
Congratulations to 111 days of sobriety :-) And Merry Christmas, take care!

Comment from 'Caroline'
Merry Christmas! You're going to feel great tomorrow!

And you know what, Caroline is right. Coming out the other side of Christmas Day, I do feel great. I'm almost flabbergasted by how great I feel, in fact. Only by doing Christmas completely booze-free have I realised it's actually do-able. In fact, not only is it entirely possible, it's (oh my goodness, am I actually going to say this?) better.

Mrs D Is Going Without (Day 112)

Boxing Day. It's so totally fine to be not-drinking at Christmas. It's so much better than fine. I'm still laughing, chatting, joking, being totally normal but without that edgy feeling like I've got the dial turned up to 9 or 10 (over the top) instead of sitting comfortably at a 5 or 6 (nice and normal).

And I'm sitting at that comfortable level while hosting tonnes of people coming and going, plus around 6 extras staying including 2 babies. The dishwasher has been going 3 times a day; we're constantly cleaning up and getting ready to prepare the next snack or 3-course meal. And all the while it's a melting pot of humanity with all their foibles, stresses and problems and, of course, all of us think our issues are the most important. A million and one dynamics and the odd tension spot blowing like a leak in a pipe.

But sober Mrs D is able to keep herself reason-ably level-headed. Not too stressed, not too territorial, generous enough with my house and space, busy but not feeling too under-appreciated, washing, cleaning, answering questions constantly. (Where are your table-cloths? Is the local dairy open today? How can I set your washing machine to low? Is there a container I can put this in? Shall we cook the rosti like this or like that? Have you another cushion for the outside chairs? Where's the hose fitting so I can fill the paddling pool?)

I've had three people cry over me in private (we're an emotional female-based family, okay?), one or two snap testily at me, a couple of them treat me like I'm the most bossy person in the world (well, you told me to ask for help), and the sleep throughout has been brief and broken.

But not once have I been even slightly tempted to drink alcohol despite everyone else doing it (except pregnant sister). Not even remotely interested. Just do not want to. Don't need it. Don't want it.

I reckon if I had been experiencing all of the above while pouring copious amounts of alcohol in my system, I'd not only feel a shit-load more tired and sickly in my guts with a pounding headache most of the time, but I'd be feeling far more watery emotionally myself. I'd have a nervy feeling in my tummy probably because I'd not been able to think and feel and process all the dynamics and interactions clearly. Happy Merry Glorious Sober Christmas to you all!!!!!

My first sober Christmas! What an achievement! I'm so happy to have got through with no booze passing my lips, and proud of myself that I managed to shift my thinking outside of just my own circumstances. Others in the blogosphere are sharing in my elation, which is super-cool.

Comment from 'Manu'

Awesome work chick!! :-) So proud of you! And far out if you can keep sober under all those circumstances, then you really need to pat yourself on the back! Wonderful!

Comment from 'Sunny'

Congratulations Mrs D, fabulous. I'm so pleased for you.

Comment from 'Milly'

Now that sounds like a perfect Christmas! You did it, chica!

Comment from 'Caroline'

Way to handle yourself with such grace. You are one cool sober woman.

Comment from 'VitalRehabs'

Congratulations on making it through the holidays in such a successful way! We applaud you dealing with your alcohol addiction while juggling so much going on and still being a very important part of your family!

Comment from 'Charlie'

I've been reading your blog now since about your third entry and cheer for you each time. You are doing a brilliant job!

Comment from 'Annabel'

I thought I had a draining Christmas, but I feel sheepish after reading about yours! You had your hands full and then some. Really happy to hear you didn't feel tempted to drink. Doesn't it feel great to know you got through the holiday and held strong? I'm certain you're right in that drinking would have only made the stress worse.

But there's to be no rest for the wickedly sober. We're heading straight away on a camping holiday with friends now. Our guests depart, we tidy the house, wrap up the leftovers, gather sleeping bags and airbeds and buckets and spades and pack the car to the gunnels. I write on my blog that we are going away camping for a week and nervously leave the laptop hidden in the bedroom cupboard. There will be no safe blogging outlet for me for a while.

We hit the road with two other families and head far up north. This holiday is about being with friends, I tell myself.

It is about being away from the city, not working, the kids having fun and the sun shining on us all week.

Two days later, sadly, not all of my predictions are proving true. The rain has been falling constantly since we arrived. There are tents leaking and suitcases getting wet and airbeds with holes in them and kids bickering and insects biting and tummies getting bugs. But there's also laughter and camaraderie and card-playing and yummy food and ocean swimming and sand-boarding and fireworks and fun. I get through it all without drinking and amazingly with no big pangs. There's just too much going on around me to spend a lot of time being self-indulgent. Even New Year's Eve isn't that big a deal. We play cards until midnight and then watch the fireworks display taking place in a nearby park. Our youngest son is woken by the loud banging and cries out from his portacot in the tent, so as one year ticks over to another I'm actually standing away from Corin and our friends quietly holding and soothing our son in my arms. Fireworks are exploding in the sky and I have a lovely quiet contemplative moment. It feels very precious. I feel very calm and happy.

The next day we all pile into cars to head away from our campsite on a day trip. An hour after we depart, in a rare silent spell in the car, something amazing occurs for me. Without knowing it was coming, without planning or preparation, I am slammed with a powerful realisation. It is, without a doubt, one of the most amazing moments of realisation I have ever experienced in my life.

Mrs D Is Going Without (Day 119)

It's funny how this sobriety journey of mine is playing out. I'm sure it must read in pretty typical fashion, these words of mine on a screen. The early days of fear and fight, the highly emotional phases, the pink clouds, the introspection, the revelations coming one after another.

All so clichéd I'm sure. But what is really hard to convey in letters and words and the odd bit of punctuation and syntax is the real gut-wrenching emotions that accompany each stage and step along the way. But all this blog can offer me is words on a screen so I'll type them down and hopefully reading it back I'll forever be reminded about the pure release that this particular revelatory moment gave me.

We were on our camping holiday heading up to the tip-top point of New Zealand to look out to where the Tasman Sea meets the Pacific Ocean. Mr D was driving, the boys were all slumbering in the back and I was staring out the window at the beautiful countryside rolling by (green grass, sheep and cows, light rain).

I was thinking about not-drinking, I was thinking about my past, I was thinking about my future, and suddenly it felt like a door opened inside me and some sort of light or a rush of endorphins or a turning of my stomach or something happened and the thought came to me. I am an alcoholic.

It was amazing. This is annoying to write because the words don't do justice to the feeling but believe me, it was amazing. I am an alcoholic. I am an alcoholic. I am an alcoholic. There were tears rolling down my cheeks. It was quite remarkable, actually. A real release. A total freedom.

My name is Mrs D and I am an alcoholic.

22

Deciding that I am an alcoholic is unbelievably freeing. It's not about outing myself to society as being a certain type of person or bravely accepting a label despite it carrying a stigma. It's not about admitting that I have a physical or psychological disease or that I am a weak or bad person. It's not about the word or the label or what other people think at all. It's deeply personal. It's just about me and my relationship with myself. It's about me understanding me, me accepting and embracing myself as I am.

Reaching this conclusion feels not only monumental but immensely powerful. It feels like a total surrender. I feel completely open wide, yet also hugely protected. It's calming and it's grounding and it's lovely.

Of course I share this personal moment on my blog. I feel more than happy doing that. My enigmatic 'Mrs D' persona offers me security, but regardless of the anonymity,

I feel very comfortable sharing with my online community. It's amazing that my blog, which is freely available online to anyone in the world who wants to go there, feels so warm and intimate to me. Yet it's not such a surprise considering the world that has responded to *Mrs D Is Going Without* has never been anything other than kind, supportive and encouraging. And so I share these intimate moments, knowing my readers want to hear how I'm going. I'm not surprised that after I write about my amazing revelatory moment I get lots of lovely feedback.

Comment from 'Caroline'

This is such a moving post. Just beautiful. It is really such a release. Thank you for sharing!

Comment from 'Sober With Faith'

We know when we know, my friend. And when we know things can change. Awareness, Acceptance, Action. Beautiful post.

Comment from 'Tammy'

Wow, what an awesome post. Thanks for sharing.

Comment from 'Miriam'

The moments of painful illumination—your post brings them back so clearly.

Comment from 'Sunny'
Wonderful Mrs D.

It is a wonderful way to be heading into the new year. For the first time in my whole life, a new year really does feel like a new beginning. Our camping holiday ends and we return home to finish the rest of the summer holidays just as a family. It's so nice for Corin to be away from the breakfast TV grind, no 3.45 a.m. alarm going off every morning—woohoo! We spend the next few weeks around home, enjoying the boys, rejoicing in the tropical Auckland climate, exploring new beaches, trying new recipes, watching movies, reading books and just chilling out.

And during this lovely holiday period I start to think I might actually be getting a little better at living without alcohol. I move through my days knowing that 5 p.m. will arrive and with it some pangs, but I use my techniques (visualising a sober bedtime and telling the voice in my head to shut up) and mostly it's not too bad. Okay, there are some days that are harder than others, but when the bad feelings hit I've always got my blogging outlet to turn to and vent.

Mrs D Is Going Without (Day 125)
So I've got a couple of gritty thought processes going around in my brain today and (surprise surprise) I'm feeling mournful that I can't have a drink. I suppose the

truth is, I really feel like a drink. I'm having to do some mental work to remind myself why I don't really (gritted teeth) want a drink . . . 'Think big picture, Mrs D. Do you want a "quick fix" release from these thoughts and then head back to that loser miserable lush lifestyle, or stay the fabulous sober reliable solid person that you enjoy being so much more?' (Talking to myself, first sign of madness.)

I feel so fortunate to be discovering that using written language is a really effective way for me to deal with tough emotions. Finding my voice, choosing words, forming sentences, adopting an attitude (cheeky or feisty or irreverent) is totally fun, incredibly satisfying, and really helps me to deal with all this big stuff. When I write something down it seems less overwhelming, more manageable somehow. I can control my swirling thoughts by committing them to type. It's not hard and never feels like a chore. A couple of days after the last one, a new post will naturally start forming itself in my head, usually when I'm lying in bed in the morning or standing in the shower. I can sense how the words will flow and the direction I want the post to take, so I jump quickly online as soon as I can to type it out. Each post only takes about fifteen minutes to write (I type fast!). I'm realising that I thoroughly enjoy being a blogger and it definitely empowers me, particularly during tough times.

I'm still slightly in awe that anyone reads what I write, let alone responds, but in the days following each new published post, comments regularly trickle in. There are some regular commenters who have been there from the start, but others drop off with no explanation and new people pop up all the time. The whole 'community vibe' is very fluid and constantly changing; however, what never changes is the wisdom and kindness the comments convey.

Comment from 'Anonymous'

Continue to remind yourself to stay the fabulous sober reliable solid person that you enjoy being so much more, and it will pass. Best of luck!

Comment from 'Caroline'

Just wanted to say to hang in there. I think all of the emotions and desires to drink are normal. It took me until my 2 year mark to finally move past the mourning loss of alcohol as well as the desires for it. It really does get easier, I promise.

My blog and my new sober lifestyle are so intrinsically meshed together that I cannot imagine one existing without the other. Blogging and not-drinking began for me at the same time. It's what I do. Tough phases come along, I write about them, comments arrive and they help, time passes and that helps too, eventually I start to feel strong again, a new post forms in my mind and away I go . . .

Mrs D Is Going Without (Day 128)

I choose to be sober. I choose to be sober because I was worried about the insides of my body having to do all that processing of wine.

I choose to be sober because it is a good exercise in patience. Being a mum is about practising immediate patience: (talking to the child) 'Sure, you can jump in all the puddles and examine the wet grass on the way to the car.' Sobriety patience is a slower and more extended type of patience: (talking to yourself) 'I just have to ride out this melancholy phase and it will pass in a few days.'

I choose to be sober because all I have to do is not put any alcohol into my body and I will feel immeasurably more proud and connected to myself. A small action denied = huge beautiful consequences.

I choose to be sober because the last time I drank I hid wine from my husband to conceal how much I'd been drinking, and if I was going to continue down that sick path I would have destroyed the wonderful honest connection we have with one another.

I choose to be sober because my friends and family are amazed that I am doing this, I can tell that I have changed in their eyes and they are really impressed (if not a little shocked still) and I look forward to showing them that I really mean it when I say forever.

I choose to be sober because I always said I 'didn't want to have any hidden shit' and yet I had a whopping piece of hidden shit which was a nasty private drinking habit.

I choose to be sober because I can! Because this is my life, my only life, and I am 40 now and I want to live well and happily until I am sitting on my porch in my rocking chair with Mr D by my side looking back over my life and feeling good.

And that's why I choose to be sober.

Getting feisty in print fires me up. I bash at the keyboard, 'I choose to be sober' repeating itself in my brain as I type. I hit 'publish' and positively bounce away from the computer with my kick-ass sober attitude rearing to go. Invigorated by my online contemplations, I spend the next couple of days pottering around my normal housewifey life doing normal housewifey things (meal planning, toilet cleaning, tear wiping and so on), never touching alcohol, and soon enough something will happen related to being sober, or I'll think something new about it, a fresh post starts forming in my mind and before I know it I'm back at the keyboard bashing out a new blog entry.

Mrs D Is Going Without (Day 132)

So I had that slightly gritty phase, nothing too dramatic really, which led to those stupid melancholy feelings about alcohol. Like that liquid was actually going to do something to help?! I mean, really?! But came out fighting in the last post to remind myself why I. Am. Sober.

Took a bit more than just that fighting post to shake the melancholy, romantic feelings about drinking, however. Seemed like everywhere there were images and scenes of happy, cool drinking. So I've been having to do more mental exercise and employ some of my old tactics to rework my grey matter and remind it that I'm not missing out on anything.

That alcohol doesn't make any special occasion more special than it is without the booze. That bending my brain won't help me deal with life. That the boozy me isn't to be admired or envied, whereas the sober me is so great.

Went to a barbecue on Friday night and did everything else all the other adults were doing: laughed, chatted, ate, played cards, lit fireworks. But did it sober and stayed more alert towards the end. Was able to comfort the Little Guy calmly as he was terrified of the loud bangs, then drove everyone home. Woke up alert and happy and made a picnic lunch to take out for the day. Oh, get me!!!

And this is the way my first sober summer holiday plays out. Family keeps me busy and we do a few social things around the neighbourhood, I hit some emotional rough patches and get a few drinking pangs and sad woe-is-me thoughts, but I practise my sober techniques and stay on top of things. I sleep really well every night, never have a hangover, and people start telling me that I'm looking good and healthy. I'm not going to lie, I'm chuffed to bits about this. I feel good and healthy!

I finish transcribing my Master's interviews and start mentally preparing for the big job I have ahead of me, which is analysing the data and writing a 40,000-word thesis. Every couple of days I pop out a new blog post, and I make sure I keep reading and commenting on other people's sober blogs (knowing how much I love receiving comments, I always return the favour). The days tick by just fine. Slowly but surely I start to see how my life without alcohol in it isn't going to be the complete boring-ass disaster that I worried it might be.

I also begin to get a better, wider perspective on the picture of me and alcohol. I start viewing everything in much more simple terms; I used to drink a lot and now I don't. Sometimes it's hard and I feel sorry for myself that I can't drink alcohol to escape/avoid/enhance feelings, but overall I don't mind too much. Sometimes I get tired and irritable and it's Tuesday and I would normally drink a bottle (or more) of wine but now I don't and . . . it's fine. I know that I'm just tired and irritable and alcohol isn't going to do anything constructive about that. I have to let myself feel emotions much more, even the tough ones which make me want to run a mile. I don't run a mile. I stay with them, grit and grind my way through them and eventually they pass.

Overall I feel much calmer and more grounded. I feel very comfortable with myself now that I have removed alcohol from my life. Every day I wake up feeling fresh and so, so happy and so, so proud.

I just used to drink a lot, and now I don't anymore. I am living sober, have been for nearly five months now, and it's fine.

23

I'm sorry but I have to interrupt your book here to tell you that you are full of shit.

I beg your pardon?

You're full of shit! You're spinning, mate, spinning the truth to try and make yourself feel better.

Who the hell are you?

I'm you. I'm Lotta from four years ago and I'm butting in here to let you know that I'm on to you.

Me from four years ago! Wow. Hello back there, how are you feeling?

I'm a little hungover actually but not too bad, nothing a few painkillers won't fix.

Now you mention it, I can't remember the last time I bought painkillers.

Whatever. Anyway, I don't believe you. I don't believe you are actually fine with not-drinking.

I am!

Bullshit. Come on! Level with me here . . .

It's the truth. The other night we had some friends over and I was chatting and laughing and I didn't care that I wasn't drinking wine.

Were the others drinking?

Yep.

And you didn't care?

That's their choice. That's fine. Look, I know you can't believe that I'm honestly having fun without the wine but I'm telling you, I am. It's only because I had to take it away that I've discovered wine isn't necessary to have fun.

Yes it is. Everyone loves having a few wines and getting merry and loose.

But what you're going to discover is that you can get merry and loose without the alcohol. Trust me on this. It's being with people that makes you happy, and a bunch of other things you're going to discover.

What like? Marathon running?

Sadly, no, though that would do wonders for the thighs. But you wait, there are some really cool things coming your way.

I bet they're all square and lame.

And that's why I'm not telling you what they are! Because I know you'll just think they're boring and lame because your life is so full up with boozing. But they're not. They're really great and they make you feel happy. You just wait. Oh, and I look better, too, that's for sure. I've lost weight, my skin is healthier, I'm less puffy, and I'm making more effort with my clothes and grooming.

Shit. Really? I thought I was a lost cause in that department.

Well, I'm still Lotta so I'm not uber-groomed or fashionable but things have definitely improved in that area of my life. I'm just better all round. So stop calling me a liar. This is the honest deep-down-in-my-bones truth. I do feel better. I feel happier and clearer and healthier and better and I'm happy to be a non-drinker.

Oh come on! Puh-lease . . . Everyone knows that's just not true. How can you possibly be happier if you can't drink alcohol ever? You're just saying that because you want us to believe that it's okay not-drinking. I think you're clinging to what those blokes Carr and Vale told you because you've got no choice, but in fact you feel dull and boring and sad and glum.

Well, I'm not going to lie and say I never feel any of those things.

Told you so!

But those feelings come and then they go. I deal with them, they don't last long and then I get back to feeling calm and content.

What about at social celebrations, parties and weddings? Aren't they just hell now?

Well, no, actually. And if you let me continue with my book I was about to go on and describe in great detail all the fun times I have over the next couple of months . . .

Can't you cut to the chase and summarise?

Sure! Went to a wedding, had a lovely chatty time and ended up in a mass sing-along with the guitars out under fairylights in the courtyard.

That does sound fun.

Had a lovely dinner out with a bunch of girlfriends, drove everyone to the restaurant and back, chatted and laughed all evening while eating delicious Japanese cuisine.

Mmmm.

Went to a hens' party! Wore a purple feather boa all night as per the bride-to-be's instructions. Had such fun chatting and hanging out with all the other women. Went to a nightclub and danced!!!

Really? Had fun dancing at a nightclub? And didn't touch a drop?

Yes! The music just made me feel so good and it was really fun having a boogie in a dark and crowded room. And I tell you, the feeling I had walking away from the nightclub and getting in the car to drive home was FANTASTIC!

Okay, calm down, you don't have to shout.

And the feeling I had waking up in the morning was EVEN BETTER!!!

You're a freak.

So are you. Anyway, then I went to another wedding and ended the night with a huge boogie—so fun! Then I flew away for a child-free weekend in Sydney with a girlfriend and had a blast. Loads of shopping, eating, sightseeing and no alcohol involved! Can you believe it?! Then I went to a gig of one of our favourite bands, Elbow.

Elbow come to New Zealand? Awesome!

OMG, I am telling you it was brilliant. I sang along to all their songs and felt teary with emotion, I was sooooo happy. And I didn't have to think about going to the bar and getting drinks or falling over randomly like I did at the Jarvis Cocker concert.

Jarvis Cocker also comes to New Zealand? So much to look forward to!

Um . . . you're actually going to completely ruin that concert by getting shitfaced and not remembering the music at all.

Oh.

Don't worry, you'll fix yourself in time for Elbow. Anyway . . . back to my list of fun times . . .

Nah, I've had enough. I get the point. How do you manage it? What's your secret?

Every time I'm faced with a night out I think very clearly about what the event has to offer, what is likely to be good and fun about it. Is it about catching up with old friends? Is it about meeting new people? Is the food or music likely to be amazing? The venue? What does the event actually offer aside from what you probably think every event offers, which is an opportunity to drink more than usual?

Is that what I do? I suppose . . . maybe . . . look, I don't want to be thinking about this right now.

Of course you don't.

And anyway, you can't tell me that aside from these supposedly great nights out, you were all the time feeling fine.

Well, mostly, yeah. I mean, there are some times that I feel a bit glum but I examine what's going on now rather than just reach for a wine. Besides, nothing ever lasts that long anyway.

So life is peachy?

Pretty peachy, yeah. Things are trucking along nicely. I'm seven months sober, I've got my lovely blog, my lovely Auckland life, lovely neighbours, great friends, kids are happy in school, I've started writing my thesis and generally I'm just feeling good. It would take something pretty major to upset me now . . .

24

It's Monday lunchtime and I'm busy vacuuming the living room. The extender arm on the vacuum is broken so I'm bent over double, pushing a short arm around, trying to clean up all the dust. I've got the music turned up loud and I'm singing along, thinking (as I often do nowadays) how contented I feel.

Corin walks in the door from work, he's a little later than normal because he was called upstairs to meet with the boss of the news department at TVNZ. We spent last night speculating about what they might want to talk to him about. A new co-host maybe? A new format for *Breakfast*? I turn the vacuum off and straighten up to face him and hear the news. Immediately I see in his face that something dramatic has gone down.

'What happened?' I ask.

He sighs heavily and pauses.

'What?!' I prompt. 'Let it out man!'

He takes his time, but eventually he speaks. Just two words, but that is all that is required.

'Political editor' is what comes out of his mouth.

I stand there stunned for a minute, not saying anything. They want him for political editor? This is huge. Corin has a look on his face which is hard to read. Political editor is a big job, a really important job, and to do it you have to be based smack-bang in the middle of parliament.

Parliament is not in Auckland. Parliament is in Wellington.

My mind is racing. If Corin were to become TVNZ's political editor, we'd have to relocate the family. We'd have to leave our lovely Auckland life and move back to Wellington. Not only would this take a massive effort but this could also seriously threaten my delicate sober equilibrium. I'm in a lovely calm, controlled, sober bubble. I need things to remain calm, as much as they can, given I've got to write a bloody Master's thesis! The university, my supervisor, all the academic support networks are here in Auckland. And what about the kids? They're super-content and settled now. We're happy. We can't move.

Then I look at Corin again and register the look on his face. It's nervous and it's hopeful, and in his eyes I can even see a hint of pleading. It breaks my heart. And in that instant my world shifts and I burst into tears. There really is no question. We have to go.

Political editor of TVNZ is without a doubt, hands down, the most perfect job ever invented in the history of jobs for Corin. He has worked his ass off to get to this point. Now is his time, he is more than ready to step up and take the role. I can see it in his eyes, he's itching for it. He loves politics. He lives and breathes politics.

And we're on each other's team. I know that this job is the chance of a lifetime. This is the big dream, the ultimate goal, right here in front of him. I know this, and this is why I cry. This is why I have to put my delicate sober equilibrium to the test, pop the bubble and (ohmyfuckinggod) up sticks and move cities. Again.

Mrs D Is Going Without (Day 220)

A few years ago we packed up our lives completely and moved cities because of a big new job that Mr D landed. It was an immense effort on my behalf, liaising with a million different people, supporting the kids through the move, supporting Mr D in the transition to a new job. I was the go-to person for the entire move logistically and dealt with the movers, the bank, real estate agents, letting agents, utilities providers, schools, insurance companies etc. etc.

I got through the whole mission with a clipboard full of pages of contact numbers and notes and lists and lists and lists.

I got through with very little sleep (insomnia kicked

in majorly because of stress, emotions and general brain noise).

And I got through with a lot of my beloved wine. I drank to help relieve the stress. I drank to cope with the strong emotions (sadness, excitement, nerves, grumps). I drank because that's what I did and during tough times, well, you drink more, don't you? Wine was my constant companion through the move, as it had been for most of my adult life.

Since we've been in the new city we've had another baby and have built up a fabulous new community of people around us—neighbours, school teachers, kindy teachers, new mummy friends, previously distant family members, sports team buddies, academic contacts, gym friends, workmates. We love our life here. We are happy in our house and we are happy in our community, which has become rich with people we love. Oh, and I've gone and gotten myself sober and am in the middle of writing my Master's thesis through the local university. Life is good.

So what's this all about? Well, it's happening again. And fast. We're selling up, packing and heading away within a matter of weeks. I feel tired and emotional just thinking about what's ahead. In the long run it will be great, but in the short term, hard work and tiring. And emotional.

And this time, my coping mechanism has gone. This time I'm going to do it all sober. This will be a test. Wish me luck.

Of course I receive a lot of very lovely, morale-boosting comments on my blog, but despite this online support, over the next week or so I become unbelievably raw and emotional. Any kind of stripped-back sober feeling that I might have been experiencing before is amplified a million times now that we are facing a big upheaval. The sadness I feel at leaving our Auckland community is like an actual physical pain in my gut. I cry and I cry and I cry.

I cry writing emails to people telling them the news. I cry telling school teachers. I cry telling neighbours. I cry on the phone to my mum. 'I'm just so *sad*, Mum. It's *sadness!*' I wail. I even cry watching people being evicted off *American Idol*. I'm a big, teary, emotional, stressed, sober mess. I manage to see through my misery enough to reassure Corin that the tears don't mean we shouldn't move. 'I know we need to do this,' I say. 'I'm just so *very, very sad* and I can't pretend I'm not. I just can't squash it down.'

He accepts that this is the truth but, boy, do I cry. Tears are pouring out of me in waves. It's very intense.

Mrs D Is Going Without (Day 230)

I have to write right now as it's 4.45 a.m. and my brain is whirring and I think getting things out in words will help me.

I think the thing is, and I was trying to explain this to Mr D last night, I think the thing about doing this move sober is that for me all the emotion associated with it is way more amplified than it would be before. It's like someone's put 'relocation headphones' on me and has turned the fucking volume up to one million decibels (if there is such a thing, and sorry about swearing but I just want to swear here, okay?).

And normal drinkers or non-drinkers or heavy drinkers don't get this because they're used to whatever their habit is so their emotional volume level is sitting more comfortably where they're used to. Only people who used heavily then took it clean away know what this is like. I'm still relatively newly sober (7½ months) so my volume is peaking and I'm sure it will slowly be turned down as I get used to living without liquid anaesthesia.

My eyelids are swollen because yesterday I sobbed and sobbed and sobbed huge gut-wrenching sobs all the way home from the university, where I'd just told them I needed to put my Master's on hold for 3 months then continue via distance learning from Wellington.

Then I cried rivers telling my friend up the road that we're moving. This woman is the most awesome, lovely, strong, kind and amazing friend and saying goodbye to her is really, really going to hurt. She is very, very special.

To be perfectly frank, I don't want to be doing any of this. I don't want to be putting my Master's on hold and I don't want to be crying in front of all my friends and I don't want to have to say goodbye to my neighbours and

I don't want to be looking for a house to rent in the new city and I don't want to get 3 fucking written quotes for Mr D's firm to approve the furniture removal company and I don't want to be organising gardeners and cleaners and painters and builders to get our house ready for sale and I don't want to deal with real estate agents again and I don't want to talk to schools and help my boys with their nerves about moving and I just don't want to do any of this because I am really, really happy here.

And all of this emotional pain is much more keenly felt because I've radically changed my lifestyle.

Corin can see what a mess I am and is working really hard to make this move comfortable for me. ('Let's get a really amazing house to rent when we arrive in Wellington.') I know he is hugely grateful that I've had no hesitation in moving us, and I can see the transformation in him now that he's heading into his dream job. He's walking a little taller in his shoes and that gives me great pride, enough to dull my sadness a little. Of course my lovely blog readers are also amazingly supportive.

Comment from 'Annabel'

What is it they say, that a move is right up there with divorce and death in terms of stress? Amplified ten thousand times if you don't actually want to move. It sounds like you're still in a state of shock. And, oh, yeah, you have to feel all of this raw and unmuted and possibly even amplified because you're newly sober.

I don't think I had any real coping skills in all the years I drank. I also don't think I realised this until I started feeling feelings again, which was around the 6 month mark. And it sucked and I cried over things I hadn't realised I wanted to cry over. And these weren't even new things, mind you. And here you are dealing with a very stressful life moment and you are doing things to cope, but still it's feeling raw and powerfully hard. I think all you can do is stick this one out and ask for help and vent as often as you can.

Focus on tasks little by little. Let go of what you have little or no control over because that will just overwhelm you. Do whatever you need to get through this, but mostly just allow yourself to feel the emotions. I really think it's an important thing to feel right now. Someone told me the lows are replaced with equally high highs and I've found that to be true. It gives me a lot of hope when I'm low.

Hugs to you.

Comment from 'Sunny'

AA's are advised not to make major lifestyle changes in the first year. Sometimes we don't have a choice. Even when it's the right thing to do, it is still hard. Getting through it will be a fantastic achievement for you.

I've just thought. Presumably most people in your new life won't know you as a drinker. So you won't feel you have to explain. You will just be Mrs D who prefers to drink soft drinks.

Damn, must have lost that memo about not making any major lifestyle changes in the first year. But here's what's interesting. I'm a wreck, and I know that it is worse because of my new sober lifestyle, yet I am not in the slightest bit tempted to actually go and buy a bottle of wine and drink it. I couldn't do that. I think hard about that boozy person I was and I so don't want to be her. I hold an image in my mind of the person I want to be and I start to realise I am actually becoming her. Raw and messy, but sober and brave. I cry, but my mind is set. I am a non-drinker. This is a test and I will pass it. Watch me.

I feel my sober armour so keenly I decide to do something external to register it. A tattoo's out of the question (the pain!), so instead I go online and find a silver jewellery maker who does pieces to order. I email her and order a pendant with a flower etched on the front and request 'September 6, 2011' to be etched on the back. Will she wonder what that date signifies? I almost wish she'd ask just so I could answer.

'It's my sobriety date, lady,' I'd say. 'It's the date I stopped putting alcohol in my body.'

25

The pendant arrives in the mail and I love putting it on each morning, with the date hidden on the back of it next to my skin. Our house sells (it's a stressful close call, only one bidder at the auction), Corin finds us a lovely home to rent in Wellington (we're moving to a brand new suburb which we know is great for families), and I work hard to get everything set up in advance for the boys (school, Scouts groups, rugby teams). 'This will be our last ever move,' Corin and I tell each other. 'Never again.'

The final days in Auckland are excruciating. I literally run away from one of the teachers on the boys' last day of school because I'm sobbing so hard. This amazing teacher has been very special to our family. It's raining but I wear my sunglasses all the way back to the car so other parents don't see me weeping. I've cried so much over the past eight weeks you'd think I'd be cried out by now, but the sadness still cuts deep. I've got no control whatsoever on my emotions. It's like I'm on a bucking bull of emotions and clinging on for dear life.

I sob as I cross the road one last time to give our lovely neighbours a final big hug. I cry when my brother-in-law brings the cousins over for their last goodbye. I tear up when the truck leaves with all our belongings in it. I sob when a friend drops in to our now-barren house to give me a framed photo of me with all my local girlfriends.

Am I overreacting? Sometimes I wonder if I'm crying tears for all the past sadnesses I've never allowed myself to feel, there's so goddamn many of them. Or maybe this move really is that big a deal. Who knows, all I know is I feel completely grief-stricken and washed out.

Finally we lock the front door in Auckland for the last time and pile into the car to drive down country. An hour after we've left the city, I'm still in a very watery, emotional state. But as the car rumbles along it starts dawning on me how much I've changed in the four years since we did this same journey in reverse.

The me back then moved cities without much crying or contemplation, with little sorrow or sentimentality, and with a crap-load of wine onboard. I boozed like a wine-guzzling maniac throughout the entire moving process. I left friends and neighbours and caregivers and colleagues with only little glimpses of emotion—I squashed it down constantly with wine. 'Byeeeeeeeee,' I'd screeched in my crazy wine-glugging faux-cheerful state as we departed.

This time it's different. This time I've done it sober, with no external, dysfunctional, liquid-coping mechanism, just my own raw faculties. In some respects it's been way harder this time around (I don't think I've ever cried so much in my entire life), but in another way it's been surprisingly do-able. I mean, I've done it, haven't I? Through a wall of tears, I've done it.

I sit in the car hurtling south and start to feel quietly proud of myself. I passed the test. My new sober state of mind might be raw, but it's robust. It's bloody robust.

I'd like to say the tears stop with this moment of self-congratulation. But they don't. I cry on and off during the three-day journey south (we overnight at a couple of tourist spots, which is lovely despite my general glum state), and I cry a little when we unpack at the other end (despite having a valet unpacking service, OMG amazing!). I shed a few tears the first day I take the boys to their new school, sunglasses on again even though it's not sunny. I'm worried the parents round here must think I've got serious attitude, wearing my sunglasses on an overcast winter's day. I feel like yelling out, 'I'm not a dick! I'm newly sober and hiding my tears!' But of course I don't.

That evening I'm walking around the local store getting supplies and I pass through the wine section. I'm struck by all the bottles and allow myself a full-blown fantasy about buying and drinking lots of red wine. I'm feeling really strung out and there's no denying an escape would be so nice. Mmmm lovely red wine. I imagine myself glug, glug, glugging lots and lots of red wine. Mmmmmm red wine.

I finish my shopping quickly, drive home and go to bed early.

The next day I'm invited to have coffee with a group of old friends that live dotted around the city in far-flung suburbs. This is the group of people we went to see on that infamous holiday weekend when I did the sad, hell-for-leather drinking and ended up vomiting in our unit and losing a favourite earring. We all met in antenatal classes eight years ago, and despite now living in different neighbourhoods, they still get together weekly. I'd been a firm part of the group until we moved away.

When I walk into the room today and see their faces light up at my arrival I burst into tears. Why I didn't grieve when leaving these women four years ago is beyond baffling. Every single one of them is a gem: kind, warm, lovely and real. We are a very special group of women who never judge, compete or compare. Yet when I moved away I told myself it didn't matter that I wouldn't be a regular part of the group anymore. I told myself I didn't care. 'It's not important,' I thought at the time. That was the wine talking, or rather that was the wine not letting the real me talk. No such emotional shield today, here I am all watery yet again.

I don't care. These are happy tears.

Eventually, thankfully, the tears do dry up. Weeks go by and we slowly start to settle into our new life. Corin is really busy in the new job at parliament and so happy to be mired in politics. I'm so happy for him and really proud every time he pops up on the news informing us what the government is up to. The boys make friends quickly and I start meeting other mums in the new neighbourhood. Everyone is very nice and welcoming. I am lonely, though, my phone is so much quieter than it was back in the old community. There I had friends texting constantly to arrange play dates and neighbours calling by with surplus garden vegies. Nothing like that going on here—yet. I know it'll come. I trust that I'll build up a new community full of lovely people. And I've moved around enough in my life to know it takes time to form real, honest connections. So I settle myself for the rebuild, sow seeds and trust new friendships will grow.

I do sometimes wonder what all the new people I'm going to meet will think of the fact that I don't touch alcohol. But you know what? I honestly just cannot be bothered worrying. I just can't waste the energy. It's a bummer. It's a fact. It's part of me. I'm an alcoholic and I no longer drink alcohol because I can't control it. End of.

And you know what else, I just can't be bothered fudging it, either. If people want to think whatever, then let them think whatever. I will be open and go along to any social gathering like a normal person and when the actual drinks-being-poured-into-a-glass moment comes, I'll say, 'No wine for me, thanks', and at that point I'll let the other person decide if they want to show a reaction or ask a question, and if they do I'll just be upfront and say, 'I don't drink alcohol, I can't drink moderately so I've cut it out altogether.'

That is an oversimplification of all the emotional and intellectual work that I've been doing over the past couple of years in building up to stopping and then stopping and relearning how to live without alcohol. But it's the truth! And if that breezy answer makes the whole process I've been through seem more easy than it has been, then that can be my lie. If I make it breezy it won't be a drama, for me or for them.

Apart from anything else I'm too bloody busy to spend time worrying what people think. I've got a husband who is flat out in a new big job (working long hours and travelling a lot), a house to run, three lively sons to look after and a bloody thesis to write. I've finally managed to get back into my Master's studies, analysing my interview transcripts, gathering textbooks, and meeting with my supervisor via Skype.

Oh, and I'm keeping sober.

Keeping sober isn't too hard. Well, it's not hard in the sense that I'm fighting the urge to pour loads-a-wine down my throat every day, but it is still hard to be feeling so goddamn much all the time.

Mrs D Is Going Without (Day 311)

Whine and moan and whine and moan and aarrrggghhhhhhh!!!!!

That's all I goddamn bloody hell do! Quit bloody whining and moaning, would ya?! Blah blah blah-di-blah.

Right. Good. Now I've got that out of my system I can move on.

I love waking up every morning. I honestly do. I love waking up with no guilt, no dry horrors, no need for Panadol, no distractions from what's actually in front of me. I've started feeling way more grateful for the fact that I wake up every morning after a good sleep with no sickly feeling in my guts and ready to start the day.

Okay, so sometimes that day contains a bit of stress or grumpiness, but it's not overwhelming. I think I have this belief that to feel grumpy or stressed, and certainly to act to others (my children or husband) like I'm grumpy or stressed, is a FAILURE. I have this stupid long-held belief that it is a FAILURE (use of caps for emphasis, is that too much?) to be a grump or snappy or shitty. That I am FAILING (that's the last use of caps, I promise) if I am anything but cheery and sunny all the time. Well, how stupid and dumb is that? I'm going to try harder to stop feeling like that. I mean, I'm also going to try harder to control those moods and not let them 'run away' on me (i.e. get way too shitty or grumpy) but if I do act like that sometimes—well, that's just life.

It's all very well understanding objectively that a sober life means having to feel more acutely, but actually dealing with those feelings is still hard for me. I've had sadness in spades, what with the relocation, and now it's stress coming at me hard out. The thesis work is getting more difficult by the day. I'm working on it every spare moment I have, and it's not bloody easy. Reading heavy-duty theorists is hardly fun (Foucault anyone?) and academic writing is definitely not my forte. It's taking a lot of effort to put my thoughts and ideas into a scholarly form. Thankfully my supervisor has the patience of a saint.

Then without realising it I've suddenly crept close to a huge milestone. Holy shitballs! One year of sobriety is staring me in the face. It's not an anniversary, it's a *soberversary!*

26

I'm not having fun in the lead-up to the one-year soberversary. I'm stressed to buggery with the thesis writing, the whole household gets tummy bugs and head colds, our youngest starts toilet training, Corin is hardly around because his work is so busy, and the weather is shit. I keep having drinking dreams: dreams where I accidentally imbibe alcohol, or where I'm shunned from gatherings for not-drinking. I'm definitely doing it hard. I smoke cigarettes in the garage and drink Red Bull in the afternoons. I'm stressed.

I think the looming soberversary is also affecting my mood. I feel very aware of my 'point of difference' yet again. All the old woe-is-me feelings I was having in the early weeks are coming back at me. I feel like the only sad dry person in the world, doomed to a life of misery and missing out. My sobriety feels all very tenuous and delicate again. I can't believe I'm never going to drink again. It's like I'm having a last resurgence of grief for the life I've left behind. My bloody inner addict is yelling at me in a final gasp to win me back: 'Drink wine and everything will be okay!!!'

'Shut the fuck up,' I bite back. 'You're full of shit. I'm bigger and better and stronger than you and I don't believe you. Now piss off for once and for all. *I am not drinking wine ever again!'*

I whine and moan some more on my blog and more than one person comments to me that soberversaries are tough. They suggest I'm mourning something lost, despite knowing it was bad for me. As always it's so lovely to get support and encouragement from my faceless online community. They help keep me strong. I can't bloody drink now; imagine if I had to tell all my blog readers that I'm back on the sauce! That would be horrendous; it's definitely not going to happen.

Thankfully, I calm down in the final lead-up to the big day. On the eve of my soberversary I'm feeling quiet and content again, and the stupid drinking-voice inside my mind has been silenced once more. Corin is pottering around packing his bags (he's leaving early in the morning for a week-long work trip following the prime minister to Russia and Japan), the boys are racing around raising merry hell as per usual, and I'm in the kitchen flipping meat patties. I'm thinking back over all the change that has occurred for me in the past year. I can't believe one year ago I was still boozing and about to make the biggest decision of my life: to remove alcohol completely and wrap myself in a warm cloak of sobriety. This time last year I was probably down on my hands and knees reaching into the back of the cupboard to hide a wine bottle from Corin. I shudder at the memory as I lay the burger buns out and start adding cheese and lettuce to each one. I think about my brain as I do these simple actions, how it is clear and sharp, there is no blur or fuzz or mind-bending going on at all. I'm right here, right now, fully present in the moment. Fuck, it feels great.

I add the meat patties and a squirt of tomato sauce to each burger then call everyone to the table, thinking this time last year I was stuck in my miserable, lonely, drinking hell. This time last year I was a sad, hopeless boozer. Today I'm not.

Roll on tomorrow.

Mrs D Is Going Without (Day 365)

Had a lovely soberversary.

Rode for an hour on the bike at the gym watching Channel E with headphones on.

Went to posh deli for lots of foodie treats with the Little Guy in tow (he chose marshmallows and one big green apple).

Had a long hot shower back home and took my time choosing clothes, laying outfits on the bed (I never do that).

Went online and bought some secondhand cassettes to listen to in the car, which has no CD player (The Beatles, Paul Simon and The Cranberries—best I could find).

Had lovely long phone call with my baby sister.

Did puzzles with the Little Guy on the floor.

Went to scooter park with all the kids after school. Bought nice takeaway coffee.

Ordered Indian takeaway for dinner; me and the boys all ate too much but was it yummy.

Kids watched cartoons before bed—big treat.

I finished up on the sofa watching the final of my current favourite reality TV programme with a mug of green tea and a piece of coconut ice.

Thought about how my life is like a pencil drawing. Now all sharp edges and clear. Before with wine it was like something had been smudged all over the top of it.

It was an interesting day, emotionally. Actually, I just felt calm and quite at peace.

Yes, there are hard times, those sharp edges cut sometimes, but I like it like this. It's challenging and interesting and ... well, frankly, I just don't want to go back to being that boozy mum who was so reliant on wine.

Mr D left a present in my top drawer when he went away—texting me from the taxi en route to the airport, telling me to go look at it. A lovely brooch, silver with wings. He wrote me a card which says, 'On your one year anniversary. I'm very proud of you, you are an inspiration to us all. You got your wings now.'

Yep.

I really appreciate this gesture from Corin (and the brooch is really stylish and cool!). I love that he's proud of what I've done giving up drinking; it's a huge validation for me that I've done the right thing. I'm not sure what I've done to deserve such a great guy and I shudder to think what my life would be like without him. And it appears my blog readers are falling for him too!

Comment from 'LovelyLady'

Oh my . . . I was okay until the part about the gift. Now I'm all misty.

You've got a keeper there! And one more time CONGRATULATIONS!

Comment from 'NeverDrinkingAgain'

Well done, Mrs D. I'm glad to know you :-)

Comment from 'AnnaBeth'

How great to be sober a year! How great to have the support from your hubby! How great to see clearly now! I live seeing things clearly now. It's a wonderful experience and gift. I'm so happy that I got to discover this part of my life . . . a sober part. You are an inspiration Mrs D. Thank you for your feedback during my journey!

Comment from 'Milly'

But Dear, you already have a set of wings. I'm so proud of you.

Thank you for this year, you've been one of my best blessings.

Comment from 'SoOverDrinking'

How he loves you! That note made me cry! He's so proud of you and look how well you're doing :-) You must be proud of you, too! I like the image of you wearing a pin with wings, as a reminder of the wings you have grown for yourself, drawn in for yourself. Hooray and congratulations to you.

A year. Man, that's a long time!

Comment from 'Sunny'

Love the note and present from Mr D. Made me cry too! Thanks so much for sharing your journey with us. May you long continue.

Comment from 'BugsyMalone'

Happy Soberversary, what a lovely day you had. Lots of love to you Mrs D, love the pencil drawing vision x

Comment from 'Miriam'

Your husband is a wonderful man.

And it won't always be so edgy.

Comment from 'FacingUpToTheFacts'

Well done Mrs D. And Mr D too!

Comment from 'MarkyMark'

You know that post I wrote a while back about crying at random times, well, reading about your husband's gift caught me off guard and now I gotta go get some tissues. :-) He did good. And you did good, too.

Comment from 'Anonymous'

Well done, Mrs D! You are an inspiration. You make me laugh, cry and, most of all, proud to be in such cool sober company! Keep on doing what you're doing!!

Comment from 'Anonymous'

Congratulations, Mrs D ... you are an inspiration in so many ways!

Comment from 'Clara'

So pleased the day worked out well for you after your anxiety leading up to it. Well done. I know it's a cliché to say 'I can never thank you enough' but it's true in my case. Finding your blog really set me on my way.

Comment from 'AdiosAlcohol'

What a wonderful way to celebrate one year and what a sweet, thoughtful husband you have. Those sharp times can be really hard—no doubt at all—and I appreciate your honesty here. I also love that you appreciate all the good stuff, big and small ... very inspiring.

Comment from 'Kathy'

Good gravy, what a wonderful day!

That was jam-packed with fabulousity!!

I, too, just celebrated one year away from the horrors of alcohol and the ruinous scenes witnessed by my children.

My anniversary was like a wonderful Academy Awards show, where I won. My son was there and I think it gave him a little closure on the pain.

Congratulations on this wonderful achievement!

Comment from 'Giordana'

Congratulations!!! Sounds like a wonderful celebration and I think Mr D was so sweet to give you something so special! You are wonderful!

Lotta Dann

Comment from 'TooMuchDrink'
Belated congratulations on receiving your wings. One
(plus!) year is an achievement to be proud of.

Yes. Yes it is.

27

Reaching one year sober feels monumental and inconsequential at the same time. Yes, it's a lovely milestone and it feels great to have so many sober days under my belt. But living without alcohol is a daily, ongoing lifestyle choice. I have chosen to never escape reality by blurring the edges of my mind. So even though the hard-out cravings have all but gone, and the big realisations have sunk in, I'm still left with the reality of the situation. And I've still got a busy life to lead, and a brain to keep tabs on.

But here is where I consider myself incredibly lucky, for I have my amazeballs blog, my personal, private, online diary, which also happens to offer me incredible warmth and support. As my second sober year progresses, despite being busy finishing the thesis, blog posts keep forming themselves in my mind and flowing out my fingertips onto the keyboard. I can't stop myself from regularly turning to the computer when I need to vent, celebrate or simply flesh out my thought processes. I blog for me and in doing so I share with others, that's just what I do.

Mrs D Is Going Without (Day 436)

Rather than whittle on about how I'm stressed again (Master's thesis) and emotional (kid dramas) and tired (lots of solo parenting) I'm going to try instead to articulate why I think it's better to go through tough feelings sober and raw, rather than reaching for a wine or five.

I could use all the well-worn phrases like, 'I just feel more connected to my feelings' and 'I feel a lot more whole' and 'I can understand more clearly' but I remember reading shit like that before I got sober and those words just washed over me. They're such well-worn phrases that they've almost lost their meaning.

So why is it so amazing?

Well, I had a major emotional upheaval earlier this year and had to pack up my life and leave a community that was rich with love and warmth and support. It was so hard and, boy, did I cry. I cried and I cried and I cried. I cried so much it was ridiculous. I couldn't stop the tears. I cried saying goodbye to my sons' school teachers. I cried saying goodbye to my neighbours. I cried all over my friends. I cried doing the dishes. I cried in bed at night. I cried driving the car. I cried so much I stopped even trying not to cry and was just an openly crying sooky mess. I cried as we left and I cried as we transitioned and I kept crying even after we arrived.

And then I stopped crying, and I kept moving forward, and . . . well, it's all gone. Not gone like I've pushed it away but gone like I dealt with it. I didn't hide the problem like filing away a bill I didn't want to pay. I paid it and it went away. Now I feel really at peace and resolved about the whole move. Not that I don't care about having to leave those people anymore . . . but clean like I expressed to myself and the world my sadness. And unbelievably that alone made it better. Nothing changed except how I expressed my feelings but just doing that made it better.

So (I'm working this out as I write) just expressing and honouring how you feel about something, cleanly and wholly, makes it better even though you can't change the thing itself.

Now when I think back to that time of the relocation and all that emotion and all those tears, I feel clean. I feel really clean about it. It's hard to explain but it feels great. Resolved. Done. It feels like I totally honoured my feelings by expressing them so openly and in a way that kind of cleared them.

Okay, even now it's hard to explain, this is a bit convoluted, sorry.

But to try and apply this logic to general sober life now,

fairly regularly I get in funky moods . . . grumpy, stressed, sad (but I am a fucking full-time mother of 3 demanding boys and a bloody supportive wife trying to write a difficult Master's thesis, sorry, just had to rant there). But instead of pretending I'm not grumpy, stressed or sad (which wine consumption used to help with) I actually just let myself be grumpy, stressed or sad and . . . well, overall it feels much better. Much better. Cleaner. It just feels cleaner. Better.

It's hard to articulate, and once again I don't think the words are doing the feeling justice. So don't just take my word for it. Try it, you'll understand too.

Luckily my convoluted thought processes are resonating with my readers, and I'm blessed to continually receive lovely cyber-hugs.

Comment from 'Fiona'

I think you explained that perfectly! I totally got it! I loved your term . . . 'clean'. I can really relate to that. Dealing with what we are feeling creates a clean slate . . . rather than not dealing with our feelings which leaves our minds and heart feeling polluted and chaotic. Loved this post.

Comment from 'JoggingGirl'

I understood and related to every single word Mrs D. It's almost like until we accept, feel and process an emotion, we're doomed to keep repeating it and re-living that hurt. Just like the bill that we don't pay and hide in the drawer, it still ain't getting paid until we deal with it. And in the meantime, they send MORE bills, then they start making phone calls, then they turn off the lights, and that one little bill we didn't want to deal with has turned into an eight-headed monster that we for sure don't want to deal with.

Comment from 'LovelyLady'
Real life is just so much better all around than drunk life. Soooo much better.

The more that I explore my thoughts and try to explain them on my blog, the more I start to understand what I've done and what I'm doing. With the benefit of time and hindsight I can see that getting sober and living sober are two very different things.

Getting sober was all about white-knuckling my way through a period of cravings, resisting urges, identifying addictive thoughts ('I deserve a wine today' actually meant 'I need alcohol to feed my addiction'), and dealing with *shock horror!* emotions (holy shit, I feel grumpy, what do you mean I just have to feel grumpy and not drink alcohol to smooth the feeling away?!).

Getting sober involved spending a bit of time feeling

boring, then a bit of time realising I'm not boring, then realising that drunk people are boring, then realising that not everyone else gets drunk all the time, then accepting that there are drunks and normies and boozers turning sober and I just fit in the middle of a big spectrum of drinking types and it doesn't really matter anyway.

I got sober, and now I live sober.

Living sober means I've started figuring out the other little things that make me feel good about myself and my life. The really little things.

Living sober means having an overall underlying state of calm, interrupted by phases of emotion that are annoying but manageable. Living sober means realising that phases of negative, tricky or uncomfortable emotion come along and are annoying, but that they pass. They come, and they go. Living sober means every time I face a tricky phase and wait for it to pass without drinking, I feel good about that. I feel great, in fact. Great in a low-key, lovely, normal, stable, reliable, respectable way.

The more time that passes the less I see living sober as merely being about not-drinking. It's also about being willing to always deal with stuff raw. I can totally understand why people relapse all the time, because bad shit does happen and it's hard! Uncomfortable or hurtful or tricky shit happens. It might happen on day 5, or day 55, or day 555, but it's going to happen, and alcohol can take the edge off it for a time. The biggest trial for me in choosing to live sober is deciding that no matter what bad shit comes at me, I will tough it through raw and not reach for any temporary liquid smooth-all.

Of course, good shit happens too! Parties and weddings and celebrations! And I don't want to miss out on any of it. I still want to go to bars and laugh with my friends and go to weddings and cut it up on the dance floor to cheesy pop tunes and I want to huddle outside on the balcony at parties and rant madly and I want to do all of that without the wine messing me up.

And I do. I always try to think hard about the scene I'm entering into, I think about all the elements that are there, the people, the setting, the atmosphere, the food, the music, the friendship, the giggles, the gossip etc. and I focus on those—those are the things that make an occasion special. It shouldn't have to matter that the glass I hold has lemonade, not champagne, in it.

At the start of my sobriety, social events were tricky because I felt so flat and odd and out of sorts, obsessed with the fact I wasn't drinking. But now that I'm used to not-drinking, most events are totally fine.

Mrs D Is Going Without (Day 450)

Sober events. You have good ones, you have bad ones. You have fun ones, you have flat ones. It would be a lie to say sober events are always great. Sometimes they're shit.

I've had sober weddings that were so awesome I danced for hours and felt on a natural high for days! I've also had sober weddings where I felt a bit flat and disjointed and like a bit of a boring loser. I've had sober dinner parties where I laughed so much my cheeks ached, and others where I felt quite removed from the jokes and like I just wanted to go home and crawl into bed.

I've been to parties where I was so nervous to be sober I chain-smoked cigarettes all night, ones where I raced around fetching other people drinks like a weirdo, ones where I fixed a false smile on my face and had no fun at all, and ones where the fact I wasn't drinking was totally irrelevant and I had great chats with great people.

Sober events rise or fall on a peculiar convergence of factors: my mood, my outfit, the crowd, the vibe, the location, the music, the atmosphere, the food, my energy levels. I've learned that just because the last event I did sober was great doesn't mean the next one will be. Nor will the last sober event being shit mean the next one will be.

Sometimes they're just not great, and I wake up in the morning feeling flat and like it was only really a 75 per cent night and then the 'is it because I'm a boring sober person now?' thoughts creep in. Then other times I wake up feeling like the night before was 150 per cent fun and 'Get me, I'm the coolest sober chick in the world, who needs booze?!'

(Driving home is always great whether the event was boring or fabulous. That fact remains the same. Oh, how I love driving home. And don't get me started on the feeling when I wake up in the morning. Sheer bliss.)

So if you have a shit sober event, don't think you need to drink to make the next one more fun. It's not about the drink, it's about all those other factors. I don't think any amount of booze in the world is going to make a boring party more fun. It's just going to make me drunk at a boring party.

I love all this thinking and writing and figuring stuff out. I love how the words form in my mind and flow easily out of my fingertips. And I love the feedback, I love my constantly shifting online community so very, very much. But I'm starting to feel weird that I have this big blog which I keep secret from most people in my 'real' life. It feels strange not telling my friends and family, especially now that I'm through all the really hard work of the early months, my Master's thesis is finally finished and delivered, and things are flowing a little more smoothly for me now.

I'm feeling at a crossroads, and I'm wondering what to do. Should I open up my blog to everyone in my life? Or should I go the other way and stop blogging altogether? One way or another, something has to change, I can't continue with this big secret anymore.

28

Of course, because sharing honestly is what I do, I float the idea online that I might wrap up *Mrs D Is Going Without* and stop posting. The reaction from my online community is swift and intense.

Comment from 'DeeDee'

Noooooooooooooooooooooooooooo!!!!!!!!!!!!!

I'm sorry, that's selfish of me, and you must do what you need to do. But I am really sad to hear this. I really look forward to and enjoy your posts so much. You will be VERY much missed around here lady!

Comment from 'Clara'

My sobriety is bringing out my selfishness! I desperately want you to be posting all the time as I enjoy your writing so much and it inspires me tremendously. You never sound like a whiner to me, just always honest and real. If you do 'wind this up', please consider writing about other things. It's not just your stories of sobriety I enjoy, but your honest approach to yourself that is truly remarkable.

Comment from 'Samantha'

Noooooooooo!! You will be hugely missed. I have loved reading your story. You have helped me to cope on the toughest of days by reading your honest and courageous story.

Comment from 'LovelyLady'

You are an inspiration to everyone who reads your blog. Your honesty is what does it ... you put it all out there and that is so wonderful! I would so miss you if you wrap it up.

Comment from 'BugsyMalone'

Mrs D ... I hope you stay here, even if you only post monthly ... But you know what's best for you. Just a bit longer? ;-)

Comment from 'Giordana'

Just don't stop writing ... you have a gift with words. You can talk to me about anything you like!! Thanks Mrs D!

Comment from 'John Smith'

Well, the huge revelations may be over, but it is, in my honest opinion, not a reason to quit blogging. Because your experience may turn out to be very valuable for people who have the same problems as you. First, you had the support of people. Now, people may need YOU.

Ouch. Oh god, this is hard. I can't figure out what to do. I love getting all this complimentary feedback and I do really appreciate it. But I'm not getting crazy big-headed about it, I'm keeping it real. I'm very aware of the fact that what I have done in getting sober is not unique; there are thousands of people who quietly and bravely get sober every day in every city in every country in the world. I'm not the cleverest, bravest person in the world. I'm one of thousands of clever, brave, sober people. I just write about it publically in a way that people relate to, that's all.

I realise the only way forward and out of my quandary is to start telling friends and family about this wonderful treasure I have in my life—my sobriety 'secret weapon', my magical, astounding, unbelievably powerful blog and the lovely community surrounding it.

I know that only by opening up about the blog can I start to figure out what to do with it. If *Mrs D Is Going Without* is going to continue, it needs to be fully integrated with my real life. I am Lotta Dann, suburban housewife and mother-of-three, and I am Mrs D, sober blogger. I need to join both bits of me together.

So I take a deep breath, gird my loins, and start telling my friends and family about *Mrs D Is Going Without*. I do it very slowly and carefully (this is a big scary deal), but it feels right so I forge ahead, albeit delicately. I'm feeling brave and strong, but vulnerable and nervous as well. It's a strange mixture.

Corin is nervous for me too, but also really proud of what I've done—not just giving up drinking but also creating a community through blogging. We talk through whether the possibility of me being outed publically as an ex-boozer will affect his career, but can't see how it possibly could. What is there to criticise? We can't see any shame in me admitting to having a drinking problem. Alcohol is addictive! And even if the news was to break—'Corin Dann's wife admits battle with the bottle!'—we feel in a powerful position. We're the ones revealing the truth, we're the ones front-footing it, we're not hiding anything. We're not ashamed. If people want to judge, let them. (And, truth be told, we also know the chances of those sorts of dramatic headlines are slim—he's not that much of a tabloid celebrity!)

So together we're feeling strong about telling friends and family, but I know that Corin is also slightly wary for me, cautioning me to go slowly and standing by to support me if I do encounter any unexpected reactions.

I'm not embarrassed to be revealing the truth to my friends and family about my sober struggles (I've always been very open about my drinking problem), nor am I worried that I have offended anyone on my blog (I have only ever written about myself). To be honest mostly I'm anxious that outing the blog might affect the authenticity of how I write and share, and in return jeopardise the genuine responses I receive from my online community. But I have no choice, given I don't want to keep a big secret any longer.

First, a sister gets told, then a few days later a friend. A week goes by and I tell another family member, then the next day another friend. Slowly but surely, one by one, everyone who knows me finds out about my blog.

They're all amazed to discover what I've secretly been up to online, and are mostly very kind about it. Some people are a bit taken aback that I've kept such a big secret for so long, but I keep explaining how desperate I was early on, why the anonymity was so powerful, and how privacy was so vital to keeping me honest and strong. Once they've had a good read through all my old posts they totally get that.

Throughout this scary 'opening up' process I keep my online community firmly in mind and think hard about all the people who have reached out to me through comments and emails. I feel very supported not just by Corin but also by all of the lovely people I have 'met' through *Mrs D Is Going Without*. There are so many brave, newly sober people online (or people desperate to become sober), reading, lurking, posting comments, sending heartfelt emails. Whenever I think of them I feel brave and strong and determined.

After the big move away from our old community, and the stress of writing the Master's, this opening up of the blog is probably the hardest emotional phase I've been through since I stopped drinking. But once again my sobriety proves itself to be robust. I prove to myself that I am robust.

Eventually I realise that integrating the blog into my normal life isn't going to spell disaster. I discover—joy upon joy!—that despite knowing my 'ordinary' people are reading (and not just online people who are interested in living sober), I'm able to continue writing posts. Not just able to, but happy to. The words keep taking shape in my mind and flowing out my fingers and onto the keyboard. I can't stop them. They just come! I'm sooooo happy about this.

And all the while as every week passes I'm feeling more and more robust with the whole not-drinking malarkey. Five o'clock comes and goes every day (funny that) and I don't have any strong cravings to drink. I don't feel any misery at not being able to have a wine, nor do I need to consciously work my techniques to get through without reaching for it. The wino-voice in my head trying to convince me to drink has been all but silenced. I can't actually believe this! I'm still hyper-aware of my sobriety but in a comfortable way, with no fear or nerves attached.

I've shifted from boozing like crazy every day at 5 p.m. on the dot, to angsting like crazy every day at 5 p.m. on the dot, to now where 5 p.m. slides by and doesn't really register with me. Forgive my jubilation but WOW OH WOW OH WOW!!! How fucking cool is that?! I'm stoked to realise that what I thought must be possible is possible.

I've proved it. I've proved to myself that it is possible to work hard and concentrate and push through and retrain your brain to live a life with no alcohol added. I've done it. And I'm not miserable. I'm just living!

Mrs D Is Going Without (Day 517)

Someone emailed me to ask how the hell did I just decide to stop and then stop? It does sound so easy when put like that. And while it hasn't been easy to learn to live without wine smoothing the way . . . it actually has been easy for me to not touch the stuff. I have poured wine for others, sniffed it, had the smell wafting across the table on numerous occasions, bought it, encouraged others to drink it in front of me, and never once since the first few weeks of cravings have I actually thought to pick it up and swallow. How come?

I do feel lucky that I feel like this. But I do think that all the retraining of my brain that I did early on helped. Reading books like Jason Vale's *Kick the Drink*

... *Easily!* really helped me see wine not as my friend but as the enemy.

Not the enemy so much as that person that you thought was really good for you and then you slowly realise that they're actually a really negative influence and a liability and that you're better off slowly retreating from that person and avoiding hanging out with them.

Like that really uncool person that you just wish would stop hanging around trying to be your friend when you just find they get in the way and make dumb comments.

I can happily fill the glass of wine and hand it to a friend because I just don't want that stuff in my body twisting my brain and sending it back into an obsessed place which I am tricked into thinking is fun when it's totally not. I don't want that shit getting in my way, turning me back into that loser (in my own eyes that's what I was) who believes nothing is fun if you're not drinking.

I actually hate the alcohol industry now for all the brain-washing it does to make you think nothing is fun or social without booze. It's simply not true. This country is awash (pun intended!) with news items at the moment about our awful drinking culture and the toll it takes on our emergency, medical, social and other services. But all the chatter is from politicians, medical professionals, the 'experts' etc. etc. ... but where are the ordinary people standing up and saying, 'This has got to stop!'

I feel like standing on the top of the mountain yelling for all to hear, 'TAKE THE BOOZE AWAY, I PROMISE YOU LIFE IS JUST AS FUN!!!' I'd probably have to add, 'AND YOU'LL GAIN BACK LOADS OF TIME YOU DIDN'T EVEN REALISE YOU WERE WASTING' and then follow up with 'OKAY, SO YOU MIGHT BE MORE EMOTIONAL BUT EVEN THAT FEELS RIGHT IN THE BIG PICTURE'. By now I'd probably have a sore throat from all that yelling but I'd just have to add, 'IT IS TOTALLY POSSIBLE TO LIVE WITHOUT ALCOHOL—REALLY IT IS!!!'

All the lucky normal drinkers wouldn't need to respond. But how I wish all the hundreds of other dysfunctional boozers like me would give sobriety a go. How much happier would so many of them (and their families) be?

Righto, time for a cup of tea after all that yelling. Bye!

Love, Mrs D xxx

29

Now that I've told more people in my 'real' life about my blog, in addition to getting online comments from readers, I'm often getting face-to-face comments or text messages from friends and family reacting to what I've written. They say things like, 'Sorry to hear you're having a hard time with Corin away' or 'Loved your latest blog, you're so right about butchers always being jolly'. At first I find it a bit weird and uncomfortable, given that for so long my blog was private, but soon enough I'm totally down with whatever anyone says. (Mum: 'I think you use too many exclamation marks.' Me: 'Sorry, but I love exclamation marks!!!!!')

The only problem I do still have is that I don't think my friends and family fully understand the whole community vibe surrounding my blog. I keep saying, 'You've got to read the comments to understand what's so cool about it.'

Sometimes they do and then say, 'You're obviously helping so many people', which, while seemingly true, is only the half of it. As much as I give, I take—I'm still the grateful regular recipient of loads of wisdom, advice, support and encouragement. And I feel real friendship with many other sober bloggers.

I start to feel like I have a great story that needs recording because everything that's gone on for me has been utterly fascinating. Not just all that I've learned about my drinking and alcohol and addiction and beating my cravings etc. . . . but also the blog! How it began and what it has blossomed into.

Given that I've just written and delivered a Master's thesis and am kind of 'in the zone' with writing, I figure I might as well jump straight into typing out all that has gone on. I start a new document on the computer and cryptically call it 'IT' (hiding it in the folder where all my thesis chapter drafts are) and begin writing: 'Holy shit, we're relocating . . .'

After a few weeks of chipping away at the story, I decide to get really brave and email a publisher. I'm thinking, 'Fuck it, I think this is an interesting story, might as well see if a publisher agrees.' I figure I've got nothing to lose—feel the fear and do it anyway and all that jazz. I go hard and write a ballsy and direct sales pitch. I might only get one shot at this so I might as well make it a good one.

Mrs D is Going Without

Email to: Nicola McCloy, Allen & Unwin, Auckland Office

Hi Nicola,

I'm writing to see if you think my blog has potential to be turned into book. I started it as a private online journal to help me in my solo quest to get sober, but over time it has become something quite else. I now get hundreds of hits a day from all over the world and numerous comments from a growing online community of people looking for support and inspiration in dealing with their own alcohol problems.

I'd like to write a book that rips the cover off my kind of alcoholism. I don't present the typical image of an alcoholic. I didn't lose my job, home or family. I didn't crash my car or fall over in public. I am a middle-class, respectable, seemingly well-put-together, successful woman who drank steadily and heavily in private. I drank alone and I stopped drinking alone. I haven't gone to AA, my blog has become an AA of sorts. This was entirely unexpected. The warm, wise and helpful comments I get from others online are unbelievable.

I'd like to go public now with a book and open up about my struggle and transformation as I'm convinced there are thousands of people who will relate to my story. I am convinced that there are many, many people who are right now locked in a private drinking hell like I was. Wanting to make a change. Scared about living a life without alcohol. I envisage the book not being a drinking memoir as such, but rather the story of how I got sober, including the story of my blog and how it grew and became crucial to my recovery.

I look forward to hearing what you think.

Many thanks, Lotta Dann (aka Mrs D!).

I take ages writing the email, checking it over and over before finally taking a deep breath and hitting send. I've got nerves in my tummy! I only have to wait four days for a reply but they are an agonising four days. When Nicola finally responds her email is worth the wait. I'm at home alone eating lunch and watching *The Real Housewives of New York* when it arrives.

Email to: Lotta Dann from Nicola McCloy

Hi Lotta,

Thank you so much for getting in touch.

Since I got your email, I've been dipping in and out of your blog and absolutely I think there's potential there for it to be turned into a book. Your writing style is so direct, so honest and relatable.

As luck would have it, we had a publishing meeting this morning and I canvassed the possibility of a book with my colleagues. Everyone got the idea straight away and they were very positive about the potential for it.

So where to from here? Well, I think it would be great if we could have a bit of a chat on the phone to talk a bit more about your vision for a book.

I look forward to talking to you.

Best, Nic

Well, blow me over! After I read Nicola's email I walk around the empty house exclaiming 'OH MY GOD!!!' wildly before throwing myself backwards on the bed in hysterics. This is another 'my life as a movie' moment. I know this is huge. A book! This will be a big step—a full reveal of who I am to my blog readers and of my drinking problem to the wider world. But I think of Corin and I know he's behind me, and I think of my online community and I'm brave. I'm ready. I'm going to do it.

You know what happens next because you're holding it in your hands.

•

In the eight months it's taken to get this book to you I've graduated with my Master of Arts (oh the joy of walking across that stage to receive my degree! Shame I put the graduation cap on backwards after I'd shaken the Vice Chancellor's hand—for goodness sake, when am I going to sort my fashion faux-pas out?!) and celebrated two years of sobriety (by drinking virgin mojitos at a Mexican restaurant with my sisters). I've hosted disco parties and pizza nights and danced for four hours straight at a friend's 40th (hits from the 1980s all night—so fun!). I've also dealt with some heavy-duty emotional shit feeling like my feet are planted firmly on the ground.

I've cried tears at various points in the writing (realising that I still don't always know how to fill the 'empty space' left by wine), gotten giddy with delight (re-reading Jason Vale made me feel so great!) and have realised I'll probably always be a work in progress when it comes to dealing with tricky emotions without reaching for dysfunctional coping mechanisms (don't get me started on sugar—that's a whole other book).

There is no happy ending to this book. The happy point, I think, came at the beginning, on the 6th of September 2011, when I made the decision to remove alcohol from my life. The happy point came when I was standing in my kitchen in my dreadful hungover state at my personal rock bottom and thought 'I don't want to be this woman any more'. Once I made that decision I have stubbornly refused to shift from it, and I always will. I will never return to being that boozy person I once was.

Boozing is living a wild, crazy, blurry, detached and numbed-out life that is sometimes fun and sometimes sad and sometimes downright miserable (when you get to where I was with my boozing).

Sobriety is not. Sobriety is not grand gestures and exciting developments. Sobriety is all the little things.

It's the lovely conversations at the end of a party, the quiet cosy conversations that are real and memorable.

It's getting up at 11 p.m. to rub a sick child's back and feeling so grateful to be fully alert.

It's the delight in an empty recycling bin.

It's driving home at midnight. I love driving home so much.

It's hearing people talk about their own struggles and not inwardly running a mile, but listening, really listening.

It's that beautiful moment after you've stared down a pang and resisted the urge to drink, it's gone away and you realise it was lying to you and you didn't want/need/deserve the drink after all. That is a truly beautiful sober moment.

It's sitting with an inner calmness that blows like a warm breeze over your mind. (Okay, sometimes sobriety means dealing with woe-is-me thoughts too, but I'm trying to be positive here!)

It's waiting, waiting for bad moods to pass, waiting for glum phases to end, waiting for the light to return. Knowing it always does.

It's really appreciating a hot cup of tea, really appreciating each and every sip. Or really appreciating a small sweet square of chocolate as it melts in your mouth.

It's looking in the mirror and knowing that whatever is looking back at you is real, not some blurry distant mirage.

It's just the underlying beauty in the knowledge that you are sober. You are not a drunk anymore, you are sober. It's that little gold nugget of truth that you tuck away inside and nurture.

I'm not sure what's on the horizon for me next, but there is one thing that I can say with absolute certainty.

I am Lotta Dann, you can call me Mrs D, and I will always be Going Without.

Afterword

Mrs D Is Going Without (Day 771)

So today I finished my book. I finished with a flourish, got teary typing out the last line, then danced wildly in my kitchen to 'Born This Way' by Lady Gaga.

The sun was shining, the music was loud, and I was kicking up my feet, safe in the knowledge that no one could see me. I felt soooooo very happy.

My book will be the final step in my integration process. For quite a while now I have had a double life ... the 'real' me (suburban housewife, mother of three) and the 'online' me (Mrs D sober blogger).

I have gone halfway to integrating the two me's by telling more and more people in my 'real' life about my blog (scary as all hell but necessary). But only when the book comes out will I be fully integrated as one. All you lovely blog readers will get the full story behind this blog. Who I am, what was going on outside of all my posts (soooo much), and how and why blogging was so amazingly helpful to my getting and staying sober.

Sober blogging is the newest form of recovery, where people like me can reach out through the internet and find amazing support. Really, the book is about you—my warm, kind, supportive, amazing worldwide community of brave sober warriors. We know how amazing this blogosphere is ... I want other people to know, too.

The book won't be out until next year some time, there's lots of editing and fiddling and formatting and stuff that goes on now, apparently ...

Until then I'll keep posting and sharing and being a part of this wonderful online world.

Oh, and one last thing ... I FUCKING LOVE BEING SOBER!!!!!!!

Love, Mrs D xxx

Acknowledgements

First, a huge thankyou to all the team at Allen & Unwin—Nicola, Sue, Kathryn, Melanie, Abba, Susin and Lisa—what an amazing bunch of women you are. Thank you for looking after me. I've felt very safe in your capable hands from day one.

To all my wonderful friends—you all mean a great deal to me and I thank you for never judging me for boozing, and never judging me for not boozing either. Big love particularly to Anna Askerud, Robbie Beattie, Sarah Cobham, Emma Hopkinson-Sneddon, Kathryn Geddes-Marks, Sarah Gillies, Nicky Levet and Katy Pearce. I'm also particularly grateful to my test readers—Robbie Beattie, Jude Wallace and Sue Kerr.

I'd like to give a shout-out to our lovely and ever-expanding new community in Karori, especially the great teachers who've been looking after our boys.

To my lovely in-laws—thank you for being so welcoming to me from the moment Corin drew me into the fold. Special mention must be made of my mother-in-law Marg Dann and Corin's twin sister Amy Evans—you guys are so special to me and your support is really appreciated.

To my three gorgeous, clever sisters: Brita McVeigh, Anna McVeigh and Juliet Speedy, I love you all very, very, very, very much. Sisterhood rocks!

Thanks Mum and Dad—Tina and Chris McVeigh—for always loving me, encouraging me and challenging me, and for instilling in me the belief that I could achieve anything I set my mind to. I only hope I can send my boys out into the world with such a great parental gift.

Finally to Corin, the love of my life. Thank you for everything, honey—everything. And to our beautiful boys Axel, Kaspar and Jakob, keep being awesome guys, and remember—everything in moderation!

Resources

If you think you might like to stop drinking yourself, here are some places where you can find help. Some of these websites are local to me; search around to find equivalent ones in your area.

My blog *www.livingwithoutalcohol.blogspot.com*. Not only do I post regularly about what's going on relating to my sober lifestyle but equally (if not more) importantly I also keep an updated Blog List running down the left-hand column of my site that links to numerous other sober bloggers around the world. Click around and find the blogger or bloggers you most relate to. There are men, women, elderly people, young, single, married, students, executives . . . many, many brave people writing regularly about their experiences in getting sober. Join in the conversation! Read and comment or just lurk; however you choose to take part you will benefit from the warmth and wisdom that gets passed around the sober blogging community.

Alcohol Drug Helpline 0800 787 797. They are there from 10 a.m. to 10 p.m. every day to listen and offer support. And it's free! Or you can text 'adh' to 234 and they'll text you back to see how they can help. Their website *www.alcoholdrughelp.org.nz* also contains a wealth of information, including a directory that lists all publicly funded addiction services. These people really want to help, so call, text or visit them online.

www.likeadrink.org.nz This is a really powerful website for people who are toying with the idea of making some changes to their drinking. The site is full of videos of people talking about their own drinking issues, offers a facility for you to (privately) write out your own story, offers questionnaires to assess your own drinking and has links to numerous resources.

www.drughelp.org.nz This is a site rich with information and support for people who want to re-evaluate their relationship with drugs, including alcohol. Very user-friendly.

www.drugfoundation.org.nz Lots of great information on here about every drug under the sun, including alcohol. There's plenty to read about the health effects, laws and penalties, dependence and overdose risk, and links on how to get help and what to do in a crisis.

www.hellosundaymorning.org Hello Sunday Morning is a great outfit dedicated to improving our drinking culture. It's not for problem drinkers, but for people who want to pause for a bit. They have a slick social media platform and anyone can join in by committing to a period of sobriety. Once you're in you can share your story, follow other people's and interact with each other for support.

www.aa.org.nz Alcoholics Anonymous is a fellowship that has been running worldwide for almost eighty years. It works by members meeting face-to-face to share their experiences, strength and hope. Members often follow the AA programme known as the Twelve Steps, which provides a framework for self-examination and ultimately (hopefully) freedom from alcohol. There is plenty of information on this site and a list of all the meetings that take place in different locations around New Zealand.